THE ROAD TO IMMORTALITY

THE ROAD TO IMMORTALITY

Being a description of the afterlife
purporting to be communicated
by the late

F. W. H. Myers

Frederic William Henry Myers, 1843-1901

through

GERALDINE CUMMINS

www.whitecrowbooks.com

Published and printed in the United States of America and the
United Kingdom by White Crow Books; an imprint of White Crow
Productions Ltd, in association with Pilgrim Books.

For information, contact White Crow Books
at P. O. Box 1013 Guildford, GU1 9EJ United Kingdom,
or e-mail to info@whitecrowbooks.com.

Cover Designed by Butterflyeffect
Interior production by essentialworks.co.uk
Interior design by Perseus Design

Paperback ISBN 978-1-908733-46-7
eBook   ISBN 978-1-908733-47-4

Non Fiction / Body, Mind & Spirit / Death & Dying

Published by White Crow Books
www.whitecrowbooks.com

"For it has been my lot to be concerned in a work more important and more successful than anything in my own capacity or character could have led me to expect. I have been one of the central group concerned in a great endeavour; the endeavour to pierce, by scientific methods, the world-old, never-penetrated veil. The movement which took overt shape in 1882, with the formation of the Society for Psychical Research, was aided indeed by help from other quarters, but in its essential character was the conception of a few minds, and was piloted through its early dangers by a small group of intimate friends. With this endeavour to learn the actual truth as to the destiny of man I have from the very first been identified and, so to say, incorporate. Edmund Gurney worked at the task with more conscientious energy; the Sidgwicks with more unselfish wisdom; but no one more unreservedly than myself has staked his all upon that distant and growing hope."

— **Frederic Myers**

Contents

Introduction

by
E. B. Gibbes

The contents of this book purport to be communicated from another life by the late F. W. H. Myers, English poet and essayist, who became classical lecturer at Trinity College, Cambridge, in 1865. In 1882, together with Professor Henry Sidgwick, Sir William Barrett and Edmund Gurney, he founded the Society for Psychical Research. He died in January 1901.

By means of what is called "automatic writing" these communications have been taken down at three different periods (1924-25, 1927 and 1931) by Miss Geraldine Cummins, w ho, in the language of psychical research, is styled the "automatist." The alleged "communicator," however (F. W. H. Myers), describes her as the "interpreter." This is an apt term, seeing that, in cases of mental mediumship, the "inner mind" appears to be necessary for the interpretation of messages and writings which purport to emanate from the unseen world.

Miss Cummins is the daughter of the late Professor Ashley Cummins, M.D., of Cork and has lived most of her life in Ireland. She has played hockey for Ireland and is an enthusiastic tennis player. She was educated privately, has had no training in science, psychology or metaphysics, being principally interested in the drama and in modern literature. Her six brothers served in the Great War and two were killed in action. She is not a professional medium. She is the author of an Irish peasant novel, *The Land They Loved* (published by Macmillan), and, in collaboration, of two Irish folk plays produced at the Abbey Theatre, Dublin. She is also a writer of psychic works. We became acquainted in 1923, and at the end of that year commenced a series of experiments in automatism.

Automatic writing has been proved to be a genuine phenomenon in which the hand of the scribe writes matter of which he or she at times may have no conscious knowledge. By this means the late Sir Edward Marshall Hall, K.C., became convinced of survival. Referring to automatic writing he states: "I was and am convinced that there is an existence beyond so-called death, and there are means of communication between the so-called dead and ourselves..."

It is possible that certain people are "tuned in" to higher vibrations and that, through such vibrations, the so-called dead may communicate again with the world they have left. I purposely refer to the departed as the "so-called dead" because it is my emphatic belief – after twenty-five years of close study and investigation of the phenomenon of automatic writing – that the dead are not extinct and that, given certain conditions, they are able to speak with those still on earth.

Miss Cummins is a very remarkable automatist. Many messages indicating the continued survival of human consciousness after bodily death have been written by her. Not only have facts been given which were unknown to any present at the time of writing, and subsequently verified, but she has also reproduced the characteristic manner of speech and the personality of a number of deceased persons whom she has never met. The said personalities were recognized by relatives when the writings were forwarded to them. Brief examples of some of these cases are given in summary attached to this volume.

The method employed by Miss Cummins in order to obtain the writings which comprise this book is as follows. She sits at a table, covers her eyes with her left hand and concentrates on "stillness." She describes the result of such concentration in these words:

"...and soon I am in a condition of half-sleep, a kind of dream-state that yet, in its peculiar way, has more illumination than one's waking state. I have at times distinctly the sensation of a dreamer who has no conscious creative control over the ideas that are being formulated in words. I am a mere listener, and through my stillness and passivity I lend my aid to the stranger who is speaking. It is hard to put such a psychological condition into words. I have the consciousness that my brain is being used by a stranger all the time. It is just as if an endless telegram is being tapped out on it. The great speed of the writing suggests actual dictation, as though some already prepared essay were being read out to my brain. But something more than the faculty of amanuensis seems to be required. Whatever intelligence is operating, it may use my subconscious mind as an interpreter, may communicate in the language of thoughts or images and not of words..."

Her right hand resting on a block of foolscap paper, Miss Cummins soon falls into this light trance or dream-state. When in this condition her hand begins to write. As a rule, her "control" makes a few introductory remarks and announces that another entity is waiting to speak. Owing to the speed at which the writing comes and to the fact that Miss Cummins is in this light trance, it is necessary that someone should sit beside her in order to remove each sheet of paper as it is filled up. Her hand is then quickly lifted by me to the top of the new page thus exposed, and the writing continues without a break.

In this manner Miss Cummins and I began these experiments. I have witnessed the production by her on paper of about fifty different personalities, all claiming to be "dead," all differing in character and style. Therefore, in view of the fact that Miss Cummins has reproduced the psychological idiosyncrasies of people whom she has never me, and in view of certain cross-references between her and Mrs. Osborne Leonard, it does not seem unreasonable to attribute the automatic writings published in this volume to the source from which they claim to come.

At the time of the first indication of his presence Myers was entirely unknown to us personally and we knew very little about him. His death occurred thirty years ago, when, in fact, the automatist was a small child. We did not endeavour to get in touch with him, neither had we read his famous book entitled *Human Personality and its Survival of Bodily Death*, nor any of his other works.

It may be of interest to describe the manner in which the following communications actually appeared on this paper. The writing of the name "Frederic Myers" would be followed by a "good morning" or "good evening, ladies." A little friendly conversation would then take place and the request be made that the final sentences of the last essay be real aloud. The heading to the next chapter would then appear on the paper, a line being firmly drawn underneath it. The contents of each chapter in question quickly followed.

In nearly every instance these communications were written without a break, and with no premeditation on the part of the automatist. Neither Miss Cummins nor I had any ideas to what would be written until the material appeared on the paper. If the "psychic power" gave out, the writing would break off in the middle or at the end of a phrase. The actual writing is much larger than Miss Cummins' normal calligraphy and there is no division between the words. Generally speaking, the paragraphing and punctuation have to be inserted later.

The entity who purports to have communicated the following pages frequently expressed dissatisfaction with the English language; showing irritation at the lack of suitable words with which to convey his meaning – to express conditions transcending those found in the earthly state.

Alleged communicators from the Unseen frequently assert that the language used by them is conveyed by thought. It is, therefore the *thought* that is thrown, as it were, into the automatist's or interpreter's inner mind, and there it finds the words that express it.

In this connection the following quotation may be of interest. It was written, without hesitation, by the alleged Myers on the second occasion on which he purported to write through Miss Cummins.

"The inner mind is very difficult to deal with from this side. We impress it with our message. We never impress the brain of the medium directly. That is out of the question. But the inner mind receives our message and sends it on to the brain. The brain is a mere mechanism. The inner mind is like soft wax, it receives our thoughts, their whole content, but it must produce the words that clothe it. That is what makes cross-correspondences so very difficult. We may succeed in sending the thought through, but the actual words depend largely on the inner mind's content, on what words will frame the thought. If I am to send half a sentence through one medium and half through another I can only send the same thought with the suggestion that part of it will come through one medium and a part through another.... We communicate an impression through the inner mind of the medium. It receives the impression in a curious way. It has to contribute to the body of the message, we furnish the spirit of it. In other words, we send the thoughts and the words usually in which they must be framed, but the actual letters or spelling of the words are drawn from the medium's memory. Sometimes we only send the thoughts and the medium's unconscious mind clothes them in words."

The above explanation would seem to indicate that communications purporting to come from the unseen world must be in the form of collaboration between communicator and medium. Obviously, therefore, the quality of the messages would depend partly on the culture and vocabulary of the mind and brain through which the alleged entity is working. It naturally follows that, if a human mind of limited ability is employed by a cultured communicator, the said communicator would experience difficulty in conveying to earth the exact translation of his thoughts.

This explanation, doubtless, accounts for the confusion of ideas and trivial remarks which are sometimes reputed to reach us from another world and which fail to convince the public of the reality of the survival of human personality.

Reference has already been made to the speed at which the writing comes. A few further details concerning its production may be of interest. Take, as an example, the somewhat abstruse essay on the Subliminal Self. The first 1,410 words of this essay were written in approximately one hour and five minutes. As a contrast, Miss Cummins's normal compositions are laboriously put together, seven or eight hours sometimes having been devoted to the writing of a single article consisting of, perhaps, 800 words.

The sittings for automatic writing occupy about one and a half hours, but on some occasions have extended to two hours or more. As many as 2,600 words have been communicated without a break in the space of two hours. On another occasion, in the presence of five witnesses, Miss Cummins wrote 2,000 words in an hour and a quarter.

Descriptions of life after death have been given through various channels, but these are frequently condemned as being too material in character and bearing too great a resemblance to the earth existence. They are, therefore, unacceptable to a large public. The matter placed in the forefront of this book also relates to the life Beyond, but it appears to explain much that, to many, has hitherto sounded trivial and unattractive. The alleged communicator particularly states that he is not infallible – that he endeavours to write of "the truth as I perceive it."

It has been claimed that communication between discarnate beings and human beings has been disproved because "all alleged pronouncements have been either ridiculous or non-significant."

I submit that the contents of this book are not ridiculous, non-significant, nor trivial. For instance, the analysis of the Subliminal Self surely refutes the claim that only matter of a trivial character is communicated, for, as Mr. Stanley De Brath, M.Inst., C.E. (editor of *Psychic Science*) writes of it: "It would be hard to find more important matter – the constitution of man in the Beyond." And again: "When the physics of the ether are better known, much of what is said will, no doubt, fall into sequence. There is no reason to suppose that the functions of the psychic are less complicated than those of the physical." Further, in reference to Part I, he states: "I think I can recognise truth when I see it, and even though I may not agree with every detail on a first reading in a metaphysical system, which, nevertheless, is a system and a logical one."

Communications which give an intelligent explanation of all the conditions of our next state of being, such as the account which follows, must surely attract the attention of thinking people. Commenting again on the book, Mr. De Brath writes: "You have introduced me to a mode of realisation which I have long desired to meet. It is something quite original and even stupendous....These communications are extraordinarily interesting. Whether they are from F. W. H. Myers must remain an open question for the present, but if they are, they will be recognised as almost the first attempt to trace the age-long progression of the human soul in the Unseen..."

Further information as to how these writings originated and an account of the cross-references between Miss Cummins and Mrs. Osborne Leonard are printed at the end of this book. These would, at least, seem to show that the same entity purports to speak through two different channels.

E. B. Gibbes

PART ONE

Comment

Existence After Death

In writing of that mystery men call "The Other World," "Existence after Death," or "Our Father's many Mansions," I am, you will understand, limited by what I know, limited by my own experiences. So I can only endeavour to write of the truth as I perceive it. You must pardon me if I seem to blaspheme, or if I seem merely to be treading the path others have trod.

We are working, I hope, for the same end. We both feel, perhaps, that if we can add anything to the sum of human knowledge, as regards man's spiritual nature, our pains and our labours are worthwhile. You and I may not have the power to bring about sensational happenings, but at least we can, in our small way, help in the furtherance of the knowledge that there are vast horizons quite beyond our perception, stretching limitless into the infinite.

These stray remarks of mine are the expression of my own "other world" knowledge. I can only retail to you the truth as I know it. Many and varied are the conditions that prevail when the soul comes alive in this world, or in one of the states to which we are subject after death. I use advisedly the term "comes alive" in connection with the soul. For the soul seems to us as dead when it lives in its body of clay as we would seem to the average agnostic. It is certainly true that many of us shades almost doubt the existence of a soul in the bodies of certain men and women of the low animal kind, who live, in the physical sense, on earth at the present moment.

1

Chapter 1

Why?

The Riddle of Eternity

Many wonderful speculations have been made about the whence and whither of man's destiny. Few have directly attempted to discuss why man was created, why the material universe spins apparently forever and ever through space, its elements ever continuing, nothing lost, seemingly immortal, changing but in its imagery.

"A vast purposeless machine." Such was the epitaph the scientist of the last century wrote of it, and in so doing he declared the faith of the thinking men of his age, namely, that there is no why. There is, therefore, no fulfilment. Matter is the only reality. And this terror, a purposeless mechanical drama of motion and life, must, with ghastly monotony, play on forever and ever.

Now, truth is far from us all; but it was immeasurably remote from those who came to this melancholy conclusion. However, if mind is accepted as existing apart from matter, there is a very definite prospect of discovering the reason for the strange fantasy of existence.

First, it is necessary to define it, so far as is possible, in one sentence. If the contents of the following phrases be taken as a working hypothesis, then we may find an answer to the riddle of eternity.

Shadow and Substance:
Matter, Soul and Spirit:
Manifestation and its Source:
God, the Unifying Principle:

3

Disintegration in Matter, in ever finer and finer Substance:
Unification again in Spirit.

The spirit, or deeper mind, which nourishes a number of journeying souls with its light is a thought of God. This thought is individualized, but not in the human sense. It is individual in that it has a certain apartness from its Creator, the apartness of the created thing from the One who gave it life.

Now, the mystic speaks of the god within him. This is an entirely erroneous statement. The term God means the Supreme Mind, the Idea behind all life, the Whole in terms of pure thought, a Whole within which is cradled the Alpha and Omega of existence as a mental concept. Every act, every thought, every fact in the history of the Universes, every part of them, is contained within that Whole. Therein is the original concept of all. So it is preposterous presumption on the part of the mystic to call his own spirit God.

These myriad thoughts, or spirits, begotten by the Mighty Idea, differ from one another; many of them, nearly all, before they control and manifest themselves in matter, are crude, innocent and incomplete embryos. They must gather to themselves numberless experiences, manifest and express themselves in uncountable forms before they attain to completion, before they may know perfect wisdom, true reality. Once these are acquired, they may take on divine attributes and pass out Yonder, entering within the Supreme Idea and becoming part of the Whole.

The reason, therefore, for the universe and for all appearances, for even the little mundane joys and sorrows of human beings, is to be found in the term "evolution of spirit," the need for complete fulfilment which can be obtained through limitation, through the expression of the spirit in form. For only through that expression can spirit grow, developing from the embryo, only through manifestation in appearance can spirit obtain fulfilment. For this purpose were we born, for this purpose we enter and pass through myriad worlds or states, and always the material universe is growing, expanding, giving fuller and fuller expression to mind. The purpose of existence may be summed up in a phrase—the evolution of mind in matter that varies in degree and kind—so that mind develops through manifestation, and in an ever-expanding universe ever increases in power and gains thereby the true conception of reality. The myriad thoughts of God, those spirits which inform with life all material forms, are the lowest manifestation of God, and must thus learn to be- come God-like—to become an effective part of the Whole.

Chapter 2

The Chart of Existence

The following statement is an index, or rather an itinerary, of the journey of the soul.

(1) The Plane of Matter.
(2) Hades or the Intermediate State.
(3) The Plane of Illusion.
(4) The Plane of colour.
(5) The Plane of Flame.
(6) The Plane of Light.
(7) Out Yonder, Timelessness.

Between each plane or new chapter in experience there is existence in Hades or in an intermediate state, when the soul reviews his past experiences and makes his choice, deciding whether he will go up or down the ladder of consciousness.

(1) The Plane of Matter consists of all experiences in physical form, in matter as known to man. These experiences are not confined to the earth life. There are experiences of a similar character in numerous starry regions. Sometimes the body vibrates faster or slower than the body of man in such starry places. But the term "physical" expresses its character and nature.

(2) Hades is a term which corresponds with the astral plane. Immediately on the dissolution of the body there comes a brief period of seeming disintegration, a temporary dislocation of those parts which make you one.

(3) The Plane of Illusion is the dream period connected with life passed on the Plane of Matter.

(4) The Plane of colour. Existence in this state is not governed by the senses. It is more directly controlled by mind. It is still an existence in form, and therefore an existence in substance. That substance is a very rarefied matter. It might be called an air of matter. The Plane of colour is within the terrestrial zone or within the corresponding starry zone wherein the soul previously had experience of a physical existence.

(5) The Plane of Pure Flame. In this state the soul becomes aware of the pattern his spirit is weaving in the tapestry of eternity and realises all the emotional life of those souls fed by the same spirit.

(6) The Plane of Pure Light. Within its borders the soul obtains an intellectual conception of all the previous existences within its group-soul. Further, he realises all emotional life within the body of the world or earth soul.

(7) Lastly, the Seventh Plane. The spirit and its various souls are now fused and pass into the Supreme Mind, the Imagination of God, wherein resides the conception of the Whole, of universe after universe, of all states of existence, of past, present and future, of all that has been and all that shall be. Herein is continuous and complete consciousness, the true reality.

Chapter 3

The Plane of Illusion

The Third Plane

Brevity can be the soul of wit, but it can also be the soul of error. It will be necessary for me to create a small dictionary if I am to give you my views, in a few pages, on that interesting topic, eternal life.

I shall first define the multitude of the newly dead, those tumultuous waves of life that break, daily and nightly, like the tides upon our shores. Birth and death are two words which contain the same meaning. How strangely they sound to me now; for I have lived so long in a state in which words are obsolete, in which thoughts reign supreme.

Roughly, the newly dead may be divided into three categories:

Spirit-man,
Soul-man,
Animal-man.

There are many sub-divisions of these particular states of grace or disgrace. But bear these three terms in your mind, for to whichever one you belong so will your future be determined. Now I could classify conditions or surroundings.

First; there is the earth life. Second; the transition period known as Hades. Third; existence within an image or reflection of the earth known to some as Summerland; I prefer to call it Illusionland. Fourth; all that life which is apparelled in form as it is known to man, all those lives in ever finer and finer bodies which are connected with the material universe. Fifth; a mental or intellectual existence within the group-soul in which you envisage and experience—but only as an act of emotional thought—all the stages of existence that belong to those various souls fed by the same spirit. I have spoken before of the group-soul and defined it for you.

Sixth; a conscious existence within and without time; the measure of time being all those lives that are passed in form. It embraces existence in the most tenuous shapes; it embraces experience in matter whatever its character or degree.

Last comes the seventh state—the merging of the journeying soul with its spirit. When you attain to that beatitude you pass into the Beyond, you realise the meaning of the word immortality. Matter is transcended, cast off. You enter into timelessness and become one with the Idea behind all life, one with God, one with that portion of His Spirit which has been connected with you in all the planes of existence.

The Memory-World

The earth is as a reflection in a mirror; it is real only through the image that is cast upon the glass. The earth, therefore, depends for its recognition upon the nature of individual vision and perception. All men, who are in the clay, are unreal, so they have power to perceive only in a certain manner that strange illusion, the swiftly rotating globe. When they shuffle off the heavy body, when in a finer shape they take flight from it, they frequently do not realise the fundamental unreality of earth. They hunger for the dream which was home to them. Then these souls knock and the door is opened, they enter into a dream that, in its main particulars, resembles the earth. But now this dream is memory and, for a time, they live within it. All those activities that made up their previous life are re-enacted, that is, if such is their will. They can, at any time, if they choose, escape from the coil of earth memories, from what I might term the "swaddling clothes" of the life after death. For all these souls are as babies, unaware of the real world of which they are inhabitants, no more cognisant than are infants of the vast whirl of life about them, of its astonishing intellectual activities, of its achievements.

Such infant-souls frequently communicate with earth when they are in a state almost analogous to the earth sleep. They will then endeavour to describe their memory world. It is almost precisely similar to the one you inhabit at the moment. Some call this memory-dream Summerland—quite an apt term. For the soul, freed from the limitations of the flesh, has far greater mental powers, and can adapt the memory-world to his taste. He does so unconsciously, instinctively choosing the old pleasures, but closing the door to the old pains. He lives for a while in this beatific, infantile state. But, like the baby, he inhabits only a dream, and has no knowledge and hardly any perception of the greater life in which he is now planted. Of course the hour comes when his spiritual perceptions awaken, when he seeks to escape from the memory-dream, when, in short, he realises his own increased intellectual powers, and, above all, his capacity for living on a finer plane of being. Then he passes from the State of Illusion and enters upon an existence which few communicating intelligences have ever attempted to describe to man.

However, to those of us who have journeyed beyond the memory-world this alleged region or heaven of the departed is false because it is unreal, a reflection of a reflection, a tenuous dream that fades before spiritual knowledge. When the crossing of death is achieved many are happy in that state of grace; but theirs is the vegetative happiness, the unintelligent content of an infant who knows little or nothing of the world in which he or she lives.

Hades

Hades is a term which corresponds with the astral plane. Immediately on the dissolution of the body there comes a brief period of seeming disintegration, a temporary dislocation of those parts which make you one. Pray do not conjure up unpleasant associations with Hades. I died in Italy, a land I loved, and I was very weary at the time of my passing. For me Hades was a place of rest, a place of half-lights and drowsy peace. As a man wins strength from a long deep sleep, so did I gather that spiritual and intellectual force I needed during the time I abode in Hades. According to his nature and make-up every traveller from the earth is affected in a different or varying manner by this place or state on the frontiers of two lives, on the borders of two worlds.

Illusion

During the period passed on the astral plane the soul sloughs the astral shape and enters into the etheric body within which he resides as long as he chooses to dwell in Illusionland, that reflection of reflections, that dream of the earth personality. Peace and content prevail so long as he remains within its borders. But in time such peace becomes wearisome; for no actual progress, either up or down, can be made in that delightful region of dream. Picture it for a moment: you live in surroundings that resemble those you knew on earth. You are, it is true, freed from money worries, freed from the need to earn your daily bread. Your etheric body is nourished by light which is not the light of the sun. It is possessed also of energy and life. It does not suffer pain, nor is it subjected to struggle of any kind. It is indeed as if you lived in a pond, and soon you weary of the limitations of that calm unruffled sheet of water. You yearn for struggle, effort, ecstasy; you long for wide horizons. The call of the road has come to you again. In short, you are anxious to make further progress either up or down.

Animal-man

If you are what I term Animal-man, in other words, if you belong to the primitive type, you will make a corresponding choice. You will desire to go downwards, that is to say, you will choose to be an inhabitant of matter as dense as the physical body you discarded when you passed into Hades. Usually you return to earth. But I am told that the Animal-man occasionally prefers to enter a material existence on some other planet in which matter may be even denser than any earthly substance.

Human beings exist on certain planets, but their material bodies are subject to a different time from the earth time, and travel, therefore, within the rhythm of that time. Consequently their physical parts are either vibrating slower or faster than yours and may not be discovered through the medium of man's senses. I call them human beings because the conditions of their lives, the construction of their physical parts, are similar to those of man.

The Resting Place on the Road

I stated that no progress was made in Illusionland. This is, in a sense, incorrect. No seeming progress is made. Illusionland is the dream of the earth-personality. For a short while after his entry into that state the soul is at peace, warring desires are quiescent; but they wake again at the time the dream is beginning to break. In fact, when these furies are roused they themselves break and shatter the dream. For in Illusionland the Animal-man can satisfy his desire for pleasure without any difficulty, without struggle; so, swiftly, there comes satiety through the full satisfaction of his paltry appetites: then there arises discontent, and he longs for a new life; he is thoroughly bored by this resting place on the road. Thereby progress is made, inasmuch as he has come to realise the limitations of the earth-dream. On the other hand the Animal-man has very little awareness of the joys of the soul. Usually, at this point, when longing for a new life with all his being, he desires that it shall be one within the flesh, that it shall be another episode passed in the grosser bodily forms. So he goes downwards; but he descends in order to rise. His experiences in the dream of the earth personality rouse the higher part of the self in him. During his next incarnation he will probably either enter into the state of the Soul-man, or he will at least be less of an animal, and will seek an existence and follow a life of a higher order than the one he led when previously lodged in the flesh.

Summerland, then, is the dream of the earth personality, so it should not be regarded as either Heaven, Hades or Hell, but merely as a resting place on the road when the soul dreams back, and thereby summarises the emotional and subconscious life of his earth existence. But he dreams back in order that he may be able to go forward once more on his journey.

The Prison of the Senses

Your present surroundings are, in a sense, your creation, in that you are mentally so unemancipated; your nerves and senses convey to you your perception of life. If you were capable of focusing your ego or daily consciousness within your deeper mind, if in short you trained yourself to pass into a thought compound from which form, as the senses convey it, were absent, the material world would vanish. You would no longer perceive it. If you were sufficiently developed spiritually you might be able to escape form altogether, though actually this is not possible until you have had numberless further experiences.

However, on higher planes of being your intellectual power is so greatly increased that you can control form; you learn how to draw life to it. As a sculptor takes up the formless clay and shapes it, so does your mind draw life and light to it and shape your own surroundings according to your vision. In the first state your vision is limited by your earth experiences and memories, and so you create your own version of the appearances you knew on earth. Understand, however, that in Illusionland you do not consciously create your surroundings through an act of thought. Your emotional desires, your deeper mind manufacture these without your being actually aware of the process. For still you are the individualized soul caught within the limitations of your earthly self and caught also within the fine etheric body which now is yours.

The Man in the Street

Men and women, as they climb the ladder of their life in the flesh, are, as it were, suspended between earth and sky. They are between two mysteries, that of birth and that of death. They fear to look downwards, they fear to look upwards: as a rule all their attention must be given to each rung of the ladder on which they seek to balance themselves. So even the most skilful among them is limited by his position upon the ladder, and finds it difficult, almost impossible, to consider what comes before and what comes after the little space of years that makes up his life in the world.

The same parallel may be applied to myriads of souls who have passed through the gates of death. Life for them is certainly on a far loftier and grander scale; but still they dwell between mysteries. They are balanced between God and their own world of appearances. So many of the dead who endeavour to send messages descriptive of their surroundings and of their life to living human beings can only describe the actual appearance of things about them, can only write from out of that limited personality which they brought with them from the earth.

If I chose to describe the Afterlife from the point of view of Tom Jones who had been a lawyer's clerk and had lived in London all his life, his mind and spirit bounded by his law-work and his own little personality, I should very probably give you what would appear to be a trite and materialistic description of the Hereafter. For, as a rule, Tom Jones is only able to communicate with human beings while he is still in a very crude state of mental and spiritual development. Usually he is like a blind puppy after birth. He writes of what he cannot see. When perception comes to him, when sight is bestowed on the eyes of his soul, he does not, so far as I am aware, look towards the earth again. He feels his own mental impecuniosity. He has not the power to express in words, which he must borrow from earth minds, the amazing character of life after death. So he is silenced, and no echo comes from behind the dark curtain which will even faintly convey the music of that other life, yield to man the strange rhythm of a universe within a universe, a life within a life, and all lying, as ships in harbour, within the infinite imagination of God.

Tom Jones represents many millions. He is the conventional worker, quite efficient in all matters connected with his particular profession, but limited by it and by his life of small amusements, by the lack of leisure which prevents him from ever considering the ultimate purpose of life. As a horse driven in harness and blinkers, so has he been driven from the cradle to the grave. His life has not been eventful. It contains a measure of sorrow and a measure of laughter. What becomes therefore of this symbol of the crowd? What becomes of Tom Jones, Mrs. Jones and Miss Jones? It is far better for us in this study of "the Many Mansions" of the Hereafter, first to consider the future of the ordinary man and woman. Are they transformed in the twinkling of an eye? Do they become great seers highly developed both spiritually and mentally? Or do they follow out the law of evolution as it is known by men?

We must first answer these two questions. If Tom Jones is changed by death into a great seer or into a lofty spiritual genius he is no longer Tom Jones. He cannot, therefore, be said to survive death. However, I can assure you that he follows the slow path of evolution; he is born into the next world with all his limitations, with all his narrowness of outlook, with his affections and his dislikes. He is, in short, thoroughly human. For such a man a marvellous and lofty existence of a spiritual character is scarcely possible. He is still mentally in swaddling clothes. Therefore he must be treated as the baby is treated in your world. He must be carefully looked after and protected; he must meet with no sudden or violent change. For he is not of a sufficient spiritual and mental ripeness to be able to bear it.

He belongs to a great multitude who must, as we describe it over here, dream back in order that they may later on go forward, proceed towards the ultimate goal, towards a state of spiritual vision when they may enter the timeless state, may pass out of the great cosmic picture and enter within the mind of their Creator. But there is much to be done by Tom Jones before he can, if ever, attain to that condition. He is still an infant needing playthings like a child, and, therefore, requiring about him a world of appearances.

The more advanced souls—whom the Church may call the angels and whom I call "the Wise"—can exist in tenuous forms within vast vistas of space and lead within it an extraordinarily vivid existence. Tom Jones is quite incapable of facing such a strange and strenuous state of being.

So we, who are a little more advanced than he, watch by the gates of death, and we lead him and his comrades, after certain preparatory stages, to the dream which he will inhabit, living still, according to his belief, in earth time. He bears within him the capacity for recalling the whole of his earth life. Familiar surroundings are his desperate need. He does not want a jewelled city, or some monstrous vision of infinity. He craves only for the homely landscape he used to know. He will not find it here in the concrete sense, but he will find, if he so desires it, the illusion.

The Wise, as I call them, can draw from their memory and from the great superconscious memory of the earth the images of houses and streets, of country as known to these wayfarers so recently come from the earth. The Wise Spirits think, and thereby make a creation which becomes visible to Tom Jones. So, in those early days after his passing, he is not cast into emptiness, into a void. After he has slept in dimness, rested as in a chrysalis while his etheric body is being shaped, he emerges as the butterfly, coming into a world formed for him by the concentrated thought of men of great spiritual discernment, for whom I can find no better term than "the Wise" or "the Creative Life."

An image is drawn from the young soul's memories. It is of a country considerably more beautiful than—but not unlike the country Tom Jones and his comrades have known. This country is not real. It is a dream. But to Tom Jones it is as real as was his office desk and the alarm clock that roused him in the morning, summoning him to his work. It undoubtedly presents a more attractive appearance than his little grey London world, but in essentials it is of the same familiar stuff from which his England is made.

Within this dream he will find his friends, some of his own people, and those two or three persons he really loved; that is, if they have already gone before him, been summoned by death at an earlier time.

Let us picture Tom Jones in surroundings that seem to him material and therefore do not, in any way, arouse his natural timidity. He is a simple soul and has led a clean, respectable life, satisfying his desires in moderation. He has spent seventy years of his life in a certain environment on earth. Why should he, after parting with his physical body, again occupy surroundings with which he is to a great extent familiar? Why should he face another existence of a similar character to the last?

In reality it is not similar. It is the period of a great and slow change for Tom Jones. His life in the world, dating, say, from 1850 to 1920, corresponds with the germinating life of a seed in the earth. When its first fresh green shoot presses upwards towards the light, then he reaches the end of his term of years, he is passing into another life. The gardener, who has charge of him and of many other little plants, places them, if they are suitable, in a forcing-house when, as I have described to you, he introduces them to a world of form similar in character to the one they had previously known.

These wayfarers find themselves in familiar surroundings amongst people of a similar mentality. But they find very frequently that their actual needs are not the same. They are not condemned to some mechanically performed task for the greater part of their existence, because their etheric bodies do not require food. They draw what is essential for their well-being from that all-pervading invisible substance. On earth men are slaves of the physical body, and, therefore, slaves of darkness. In the Hereafter we may truly say that, given certain conditions, they become servants of the light. As food, or its equivalent money, is not the principal object of their existence, they have at last time to serve the light. That is to say, they are in a position in which they can reflect at their leisure and begin to reach towards this strange and marvellous life of the mind.

Now, with the dissolution of the body, at least one desperate clamorous need has gone from us. We do not any longer require the three or four meals a day that were of such excessive importance. One primal factor in earth-life is eliminated, and that is hunger. But we have other factors of great importance to consider. After hunger there comes sex. Has this need also disappeared with the dissolution of the body?

I think my answer, in most cases, should be in the negative. It has not disappeared, but it is changed. And here we come face to face with one of the great problems in this period of transition.

First, it is necessary to attempt some definition of sexual desire. It takes many forms. Some of these are perverted. Let us deal with these perversions, and, in so doing, we shall deal with what man calls sin. Cruelty perhaps cuts more deeply into human nature than any other sex perversion. It marks the human soul, scars it more deeply than almost any other vice. The cruel man who has changed his natural craving for affection into a longing to give pain to others necessarily finds himself in a world here where he cannot satisfy this craving. He has pandered to it during all his earth life, and so it has become an integral part of his soul. In the new life he has not, for a time at any rate, the power to inflict pain on anything living. This means for him, with his greatly increased mental powers, a very terrible distress. He goes about seeking whom he may devour and finding naught. The misery of such an unsatisfied state is largely of a mental character. What use to him is a world of light and beauty while still this foul earth longing is unsatisfied? For him there is only one release from his mental purgatory. And until he can find a way of escape, until there is an actual change in his cold, cruel soul, he will remain in outer darkness.

Christ spoke of that outer darkness as being the lot of sinners. By this saying, He did not imply darkness as we know it—the darkness recognized by the senses. He meant a darkness of soul, a mental distress, a perverted desire that cannot find its satisfaction.

Eventually this individual faces up to his own misery, to his vice; and then the great change comes. He is put in touch with a portion of the Great Memory which Saint John has called the *Book of Life*. He becomes aware of all the emotions roused in his victims by his acts. He enters into a small part of the mighty Superconscious Memory of his generation which hovers near the earth. No pain, no anguish he has caused has perished. All has been registered, has a kind of existence that makes him sensible of it once he has drifted into touch with the web of memory that clothed his life and the lives of those who came into contact with him on earth.

The history of the cruel man in the Hereafter would make a book which I am not permitted to write. I can only briefly add that his soul or mind becomes gradually purified through his identification with the sufferings of his victims.

I have wandered away from the theme of Tom Jones in order to explain what is meant by Christ's statement that the sinner is cast into outer darkness where there is wailing and gnashing of teeth. It is a mental darkness into which the sinner plunges. His own perverted

THE PLANE OF ILLUSION

nature has drawn this suffering upon himself. He had free will, the power to choose, and, temporarily at any rate, he chose this mental darkness in the Afterlife.

Now, I would give you one more illustration. Let us take for example a man, or if you prefer a woman, who has led an immoral life on earth. Here I may borrow a saying of the angel who appeared to John: "He that is filthy let him be filthy still." (Rev. xxii. 11) The man who comes into this life with a sex history of a reprehensible kind finds, when he enters the Kingdom of the Mind, that as his mental perceptions are sharpened so his predominant earth-desire is intensified, his mental power being far more considerable. He can, at will, summon to himself those who will gratify this over-developed side of his nature. Others of his kind gravitate to him. And for a time these beings live in a sex paradise. But bear in mind that it is created by their mental "make-up," by their memories and their imagination. They yearn still for gross sensation, not for that finer life, which is the spirit of sexual love, that perfect comradeship without the gratification of the grosser feelings.

They obtain it in abundance, and there follows a horrible satiety. They come to loathe what they can obtain in excess and with ease; and then they find it extraordinarily difficult to escape from those who share these pleasures with them.

A murderer comes into the category of such men. It is a sudden perverted desire, a lust for cruelty which leads in many cases to murder.

The last state in Illusionland might be termed the purgatorial state.' Obviously, it is extremely painful to realise the misery of satiety, to come to the end of the desired pleasure. There is one greater misfortune than the non-realization of the heart's desire and that is its realization. For human beings are so constituted that they are almost invariably seeking a false dream, a will-o'-the-wisp, and no permanent content can be obtained from its fulfilment.

It is, of course, impossible to lay down an iron rule. Each individual has a different experience from each other individual in Hades and Illusionland. In certain cases he is not given the power to satisfy his desires. Actually, he is able to do so, but his own ego does not permit such satisfaction. For instance, the cold selfish man in Illusionland may dwell in darkness, for it is not within the power of his ego to throw itself outwards, to express itself in the fantasy of fulfilled desires. He is thrown more than ever inwards by the shock of death. He believes he has lost everything. He loses contact with all except the sense of his own thinking existence. A nightmare of darkness prevails for a time, prevails as long as he lives within his morbid sense of loss, within his desire, which is merely to gratify himself without any regard for others. There may be only night in Illusionland for the abnormally selfish man.

Nearly every soul lives for a time in the state of illusion. The large majority of human beings when they die are dominated by the conception that substance is reality, that their particular experience of substance is the only reality. They are not prepared for an immediate and complete change of outlook. They passionately yearn for familiar though idealized surroundings. Their will to live is merely to live, therefore, in the past. So they enter that dream I call Illusionland. For instance, Tom Jones, who represents the unthinking man in the street, will desire a glorified brick villa in a glorified Brighton. So he finds himself the proud possessor of that twentieth-century atrocity. He naturally gravitates towards his acquaintances, all those who were of a like mind. On earth he longed for a superior brand of cigar. He can have the experience *ad nauseam* of smoking this brand. He wanted to play golf, so he plays golf. But he is merely dreaming all the time or, rather, living within the fantasy created by his strongest desires on earth.

After a while this life of pleasure ceases to amuse and content him. Then he begins to think and long for the unknown, long for a new life. He is at last prepared to make the leap in evolution and this cloudy dream vanishes.

Chapter 4

Consciousness

On earth, consciousness is as a lamp lit each morning when you awake. If you are in poor health the flame is feeble, if you are young and vigorous it flares up and seems to illumine every material object you meet, giving to it a special and happy radiance.

This daily consciousness changes according to age and experience. From one year's end to another it is never quite the same, though you probably do not note its almost imperceptible changes. It is the ego which sees, touches, hears and is aware of the material world. I have already told you that this fantastic being is a sum in arithmetic. After death, and after the stages of transition, that ego, with certain important changes, again resumes its sway. Whatever the plane of being on which it arrives, it is now a traveller who has discarded flesh and blood, the brain cells, the intricate web of nerves which brought unity and proportion to the body, which made of it a kingdom. In its place there is a very much finer shape. This shape also possesses its means of communication, and these feed the whole of the new structure of very subtle atoms. It is, as I have said, a structure so rare, so fine, that it is invisible to the mortal eye and eludes the finest instruments of the scientists.

Actual pain is not felt in any of the parts of this new image of man. For now the mind has greatly increased powers, and though it may experience pain in the spiritual or intellectual sense, such is its control of its outward form on the Fourth Plane that form cannot hurt it in the earthly or physical sense, cannot be, in any respect, the ruler. You will realise, therefore, that an important advance has been made. On the other hand, man has still to pass through many states, to experience numberless lives before he draws near the goal, before he reaches out towards fulfilment.

Roughly, I may define his consciousness for the greater part of his journey as follows: spirit or higher soul, ego or lower soul, and their manifestation in form.

There is also what I might call the ladder of consciousness. The rungs of the ladder represent the various lives from the alleged beginning to the final achievement; though it is not for me to say that there is any finality. When I use the term "final" I merely desire to indicate the limits of my vision. Now the soul or ego is the actual self or surface awareness on each rung of the ladder; the spirit is the light from above. It illumines every rung of the ladder, embraces the whole. The soul, then, is merely the part, the gatherer of experience, the representative of the mystery behind all life.

The higher the ego climbs on the ladder of consciousness, the nearer it draws to other kindred souls. I have already told you that there may be a thousand, a hundred, or merely twenty souls all fed by one spirit. Their consciousness of comrade-souls increases on the higher levels of existence. In time they are able to enter into the other souls' memories, perceive their experiences and be sensible of them as if they were theirs. Mind becomes communal in the last stages, for the spirit, the unifying principle, is tending all the time to produce greater harmony, and therefore greater unity. These various individuals are merging more and more, becoming one in experience and in mind, and thus attaining to undreamt-of levels of intellectual power.

On the lower rungs of this ladder of consciousness dwell those souls who still cling to human habits of thought, to the earthly personality, to their own individual line of thought. On earth some of them have been extremely learned. But knowledge does not make a wise man. A great Indian Yogi, a Chinese sage, a learned or holy Christian father may dwell for aeons of time within the Third and Fourth Super-terrestrial States. They are typical representatives of Soul-man, and they have his short-comings. They cling to the line of thought which was theirs on earth, and so they remain sadly individualized in it; they are caught in its dream, and are snared in the many errors thereof. For instance the Indian Yogi and the Chinese sage may still seek only to follow the aspiration of their particular religion or philosophy, the freeing of the soul from matter, ecstatic contemplation of the universe.

They appear to gain their aspiration; but in consequence they abide merely on one of the lower rungs of the ladder. They believe that they have attained to Nirvana, that they have passed out Yonder—entered into the Mystery of God. But they have done nothing of the kind; for they are still individualized, still clinging to their blissful little dream created when they were on earth. They are living in the stagnant pond. They are progressing neither up nor down. They have no contact with the material aspect of the universe, and their state of alleged ecstatic contemplation narrows and limits experience, confines them still in the prison of their own ego.

I remarked before that when souls reached to the higher rungs of the ladder they became merged in the unifying Spirit, and might at last journey out Yonder, enter into the Mystery of God. In so doing they slough form and no longer express themselves in an outward appearance. But those spirits who pass out Yonder do not dwell in ecstatic contemplation as does the sage or the Yogi, they are, though formless, in contact with the whole of the material universe: an incredible activity of a spiritual and intellectual kind is theirs. For now they share in the timeless Mystery; now they are in the true Nirvana, in the highest Christian Heaven; they know and experience the alpha and omega of the material universe. The chronicle of all planetary life, the history of the earth from the beginning to the end are theirs. Truly they are not merely heirs, they have become inheritors, in deed and in truth, of eternal life. You are, as you climb the long ladder of consciousness, a sum in arithmetic. When you pass out Yonder you become the Whole.

The spirit, which lights up the ladder, is an individualized thought of God, a thought that may dwell within its own life, or that may still be in intense and direct contact with God when that thought contacts directly the human ego. A Spirit-man is a human being—of whom perhaps a few score have appeared on earth since time began. He differs from others in that his spirit retains that intense and direct inspiration from God when it enters into time and communicates with the incarnate man. Therefore, Spirit-man alone has expressed eternal truth, either in his life or in his words. When his physical body dies he dwells in Hades, but he does not tarry in Illusionland. Swiftly he passes up the rungs of the ladder; easily may he become one with the Father. For even while on earth he has known the Father, having drawn his inspiration from the imagination of God.

Chapter 5

The Plane of Colour

The Fourth Plane

The Soul-Man—The Breaking of the Image

In Illusionland you wear an etheric body. It is of a finer or more tenuous matter than the physical form. If you belong to the second class, if you are a Soul-man—in other words an intelligent, ethically developed soul—you will desire to go up the ladder of consciousness. The longing for a physical existence will have been burned into ashes with, however, a few exceptions.

Certain Soul-men desire to return to earth, or wish, at any rate, for some planetary existence wherein they may achieve some intellectual triumph, or wherein they may play a notable part in the strife of earthly or planetary life. These, then, become incarnate again. But the majority of Soul-men slough their etheric body and put on a shape which is a degree finer. They are then released from Illusionland, from that nursery in which they merely lived in the old fantasy of earth.

Now, these beings wear a subtle body and they enter a world I would call Super-terrestrial; for they still abide within the ether. Ether is a bad term; but I cannot find another word to define that air or, I would rather say, fluid or emanation which is of the material universe. Pray remember that ether is the ancestor of matter as you know it. But I am wandering from my theme.

As long as Soul-man would live mainly in form, he must be content to be a Super-terrestrial being. That state contains many degrees, many vehicles of expression. They differ in the rates of vibration; the finer they are, the greater your spiritual and intellectual perceptions; the wider your grasp, the loftier your experience of that Mystery we call God—the goal of all spiritual attainment.

Now, in the state beyond Illusion, when you are living consciously and are sensible of your subtle body, you dwell in a world which is the original of the earth. Briefly, the earth is an ugly smudged copy of the world wherein dwells the subtle soul in its subtle body. You are doubtless aware' that the copyist, when he produces his painting of a masterpiece, usually fails through being unable to convey the soul of the work in question. The measurements may be correct, colouring and line excellent, but the life is not within it; so you are left cold and aloof, you are merely stirred to a petty irritation when you perceive a copy of an old master you loved. The earth, as you know it, is this unreal thing— a copy of a masterpiece. It is a shadow with all the defects of a shadow. It is, at times, distorted and grotesque; at times, a mere dim outline. Animation is absent. The true life is not expressed in it.

Within the subtle world of which I speak you will perceive a variety of forms which are not known on earth and therefore may not be expressed in words. Yet there is a certain similarity, a correspondence between the appearances of nature and the appearances on this luminiferous plane. Flowers are there; but these are in shapes unknown to you, exquisite in colour, radiant with light. Such colours, such lights are not contained within any earthly octave, are expressed by us in thoughts and not in words. For, as I previously remarked, words are for us obsolete. However, the soul, in this plane of consciousness, must struggle and labour, know sorrow but not earth sorrow, know ecstasy but not earth ecstasy. The sorrow is of a spiritual character, the ecstasy is of a spiritual kind. These two transcend imagination, but they finally lead the soul to the borders of the Super-terrestrial region.

A Chapter in Superlatives—The Apotheosis of Form

The soul becomes possessed of a new awareness as well as of finer perceptions when he decides to go upwards rather than downwards on the ladder of consciousness; and, therefore, he enters the Fourth plane of being.

On earth the average man's normal ego is largely controlled by the body's desires, though the spirit inspires its life and at times lights up the darkness of the human brain with luminous flashes. Still, the spirit,

THE PLANE OF COLOUR

or what I call the deeper mind, can only faintly impress itself upon the ego. Now, in the Fourth stage the spirit is able to enter, with greater intensity, into the time measurement which I call the soul or ordinary consciousness. This soul becomes sensible of the change through his greatly increased intellectual powers. With that increased awareness there comes greater concentration. The memory of the earth life, in its details, is for the time being lost. As long as the soul dwells in form he is subject to the rhythm of the universe and, therefore, to some form of time. Conceive time and appearance as one symbol.

The soul bears with him, however, the fundamental emotional memory, or rather retains contact with it in the first stage on the Fourth plane of life. This plane of colour might be more aptly termed "The Breaking of the Image." For on this level of consciousness the soul learns how to control form, learns by myriad experiences the ghostliness of all substance. In the anterior period of his evolution he has been controlled largely by substance. Slowly the graven image is broken, slowly the ego learns so to draw from the higher soul or spirit that he can, at will, break up his form and break from all forms, all appearances about him.

Of course, each individual's experiences vary enormously. I take as my example a sensitive Soul-man who makes definite progress upwards, who does not, as do so many, journey with the undulatory motion of a sea wave, up and down, up and down, though always reaching a little in higher than before.

Now this sensitive Soul-man realises first of all that he has entered a world of myriad colours, lights and sounds. He is sensible of a body entirely dissimilar from the human body. As regards appearance, it can only be described as being apparently a compound of light and colours unimaginable. The shape of this form is influenced by all the ego's past acts so far as they have impressed themselves on his deeper consciousness. This coloured compound may be grotesque, bizarre in form, may be lovely beyond words, may possess strange absurdities of outline, or may transcend the loftiest dream of earthly beauty.

In this many-coloured region the form vibrates with extreme intensity, for now mind expresses itself more directly in form: so that we can hear the thoughts of other souls. At first only one at a time may break upon that hearing. But after a while we become sensible of the fact that we may hear the thoughts of several souls, each apart and distinct from the other. We dwell in a world of appearances in some respects similar to the earth. Only all this vast region of appearances is gigantic in conception, terrifying and exquisite according to the manner in which it presents itself to the Soul-man. It is far more fluidic, less apparently solid than earth surroundings.

This many-coloured world is nourished by light and life in a greater purity, vibrates at an unimaginable speed. The souls, who dwell within the first zone, realise that with increased consciousness they have gained a far greater sensitivity. A hostile Soul-man's mentality may, with a powerful projection of thought, blast and wither some part of your body of light and colour. You have to learn how to send out protecting rays. If on earth some other man or woman was your enemy and you hated one another bitterly, you will encounter this man or woman on this luminiferous plane; the old emotional memory will awaken when you meet. For love and hate draw you inevitably towards those souls who are in the pattern of your particular design which is ever shaping and reshaping in the tapestry of eternity.

You will understand, therefore, that pain and pleasure, joy and despair are once more experienced. Again, however, they differ greatly from the earthly conception of them; they are of a finer quality, of an intellectualised character. Mightier is their inspiration, more profound the despair they arouse, inconceivable the bliss they stir within the deeps of your being.

On this luminiferous plane the struggle increases in intensity, the efforts expended are beyond the measure of earthly experience. But the results of such labour, of such intellectualised and spiritualised toil and battle also transcend the most superb emotion in the life of man. In brief, all experience is refined, heightened, intensified, and the actual zest of living is increased immeasurably.

Awareness on the Fourth Plane

The preceding remarks, outlining a more rarefied existence in the Super-terrestrial zone, must be regarded as merely a rough tracing of a very varied state of being. For instance, in that more spiritualised state there are many forms of expression. In it the soul wears several bodies, passing from one to another as he advances. These become more and more subtle indeed, the fineness of their texture cannot be grasped or understood by even a super-scientist. One law prevails, however, your soul is only aware of those beings who possess bodies vibrating with the same intensity—that is, unless he puts himself into a state analogous to that strange sleep known as hypnosis. When thus conditioned he may go back, temporarily descend a rung of the ladder and make mental contact with a soul who inhabits a denser shape. He can even descend into Hades, enter its fog and come into touch with human beings. He is thereby frequently caught in the dream of the earth's personality; and it is as if the memory of his experiences on a higher plane were temporarily anaesthetised away. So he is incapable of conveying to earth— save with rare exceptions—any interesting or remarkable information. Caught in the cocoon of earth memories, which frequently are not his own, he can merely speak of trivial material affairs. It is as if he were a drugged bee in a hive, a bee sated with honey.

His awareness on the luminiferous plane has vastly increased, but usually he cannot convey a sense of it to those individuals he may endeavour to contact if he chooses once more, like Orpheus, to go down into Hell in search of the beloved. These remarks will explain why so few ever receive any spontaneous impression of the departed. Indeed, men and women are as ghosts to us, and only when they seek us with faith and with love do they obtain any convincing suggestion of ourselves, of our earth personality. Such a search is legitimate and will neither hurt nor distress the one who is summoned or sought.

Now, a human being cannot imagine a new sound, a new colour or feeling; so it is impossible for him to conceive the infinite variety of new sounds, colours and feelings experienced by us on the Fourth stage, which I have called "The Breaking of the Image."

Nearly half of the earth life is passed in sleep, that is to say, in a state of unconsciousness; and it is calculated that even when man is awake, his normal healthy self, his consciousness is broken by gaps of unconsciousness forty or fifty to a second.

In this respect he resembles* a light house that stands upon a rocky coast on a starless night. Darkness impenetrable covers the sea; every now and then it is lit up by a ray of light which flashes across the waters, illumining their surface but feebly and momentarily. Man's consciousness appears thus to me now. In his journey up the ladder he is gradually emerging from that darkness in the sense that the light

---

* An interesting corroboration of this somewhat startling calculation appears as a footnote to page 328 of E. D. Fawcett's *The Individual and Reality*. It is as follows: "The reference is not merely to sleep, etc. It has been calculated (by whom I cannot recall) that consciousness is broken by unconscious gaps no less than fifty times a second." E. B. G.

becomes brighter, more continuous. When he reaches the Fourth stage his awareness is as brilliant as an ordinary man's awareness is feeble. There are far fewer gaps of unconsciousness, for the spirit can make a surer and more consistent contact with the soul by reason of the fineness of its body and its greater subtlety, by reason of increased intellectual activity on his part. The blind puppy is beginning to open his eyes at last.

Pray examine the picture of the night sea again. It is almost continually illumined by the beacon of the lighthouse. Only at long intervals does darkness descend. Now how is it possible to convey to human beings, by the primitive rude sounds called words, the implications that arise from this far greater awareness? For instance, the intensity of the thought processes of the emotional life seem limitless when compared with the sluggish movements of the human brain, with the crude passion that is roused in the stirring moments of earth life. Take the intellectual activity of a slug or a snail, compare it with that of a man and you will understand how different is the mental world of the soul on the Fourth plane from that of the human being.

Our conception of space differs entirely from yours. I can give you a faint glimpse of it if I use the wireless message as an illustration. I have but to concentrate my thought for what you might call a moment and I can build up a likeness of myself, send that likeness speeding across our vast world to a friend, to one, that is, in tune with me. Instantly I appear before that friend though I am remote from him; and my likeness holds speech—in thought, remember, not words—with this friend. Yet, all the time, I control it from an enormous distance; and as soon as the interview is concluded I withdraw the life of my thought from that image of myself, and it vanishes. Of course, I can only make this contact with those on my plane who are familiar with me and, therefore, are in my rhythm.

This trivial illustration of the power of thought to give reality to itself is mentioned here merely in order to show you how much nearer we have come to the Creative Principle. We are gradually learning how to live within and without form, learning how ghostly is the most tenuous substance. We are becoming aware of the fluid, flowing character of mind. We understand how it can control energy and life-force, those units which nourish all manifestations and appearances.

Chapter 6

The Group-Soul

The Group of Psychic Consciousness
The Physical Body: A Group of Atomic Consciousness

The group-soul is one and yet many. The informing spirit makes these souls one. I think I have explained to you before, that as there are certain centres in the brain, so in psychic life there are a number of souls all bound together by one spirit, depending for their nourishment on that spirit.

When I was on earth I belonged to a group-soul, but its branches and the spirit—which might be compared to the roots—were in the invisible. Now, if you would understand psychic evolution, this group-soul must be studied and understood. For instance, it explains many of the difficulties that people will assure you can be removed only by the doctrine of reincarnation. You may think my statement frivolous, but the fact that we do appear on earth to be paying for the sins of another life is, in a certain sense, true. It was our life, and yet not our life. In other words, a soul belonging to the group of which I am a part lived that previous life which built up for me the framework of my earthly life, lived it before I had passed through the gates of birth.

In this invisible world there is infinite variety of conditions. I can only speak of what I know. I do not claim to be infallible. Take the following as the axiom I would lay down for you.

Many Soul-men do not seek another earth life, but their spirit manifests itself many times on earth and it is the bond which holds together a group of souls, who, in the ascending scale of psychic evolution, act and react upon one another. So, when I talk of my spiritual forbears I do not speak of my physical ancestors, I speak of those soul-ancestors who are bound to me by one spirit. There may be contained within that spirit twenty souls, a hundred souls, a thousand souls. The number varies. It is different for each man. But what the Buddhists would call the karma I had brought with me from a previous life is, very frequently, not that of my life, but of the life of a soul that preceded me by many years on earth and left for me the pattern which made my life. I, too, wove a pattern for another of my group during my earthly career. We are all of us distinct, though we are influenced by others of our community on the various planes of being.

When your Buddhist speaks of the cycle of births, of man's continual return to earth, he utters but a half-truth. And often half a truth is more inaccurate than an entire misstatement. I shall not live again on earth, but a new soul, one who will join our group, will shortly enter into the pattern or karma I have woven for him on earth. No doubt "karma" is a word I use incorrectly here. For it is something more and something less than karma that he inherits. I am, therefore, a kingdom, and yet I am but a unit in that kingdom.

You may say to me that, for the Soul-man, one earth life is not enough. But, as we evolve here, we enter into those memories and experiences of other lives that are to be found in the existence of the souls that preceded us, and are of our group.

I do not say that this theory, which I offer you, can be laid down as a general rule. But undoubtedly it is true in so far as it is what I have learned and experienced.

Now, this speculation—as you would probably call it—is interesting when applied to genius. The souls who have preceded us on earth naturally stamp us mentally and morally. If a certain type of psyche is continually being evolved in the one group, you will find that eventually that type, if it be musical, will have a musical genius as its representative on earth. It will harvest all the tendencies in those vanished lives, and it will then have the amazing unconscious knowledge that is the property of genius.

Here, in the After-death, we become more and more aware of this group-soul as we make progress. Eventually we enter into it and share the experiences of our brethren. You must understand, therefore, that existence for my soul-as separate and apart from my individual ego—is dual. I lived two lives, one in the world of form, and one subjective, in the community of which I am a member.

Men and women may not care to accept these statements of mine. They long either for an indestructible individuality in the Hereafter or for a kind of spiritual swoon in the life of God. You will perceive in my analysis of the group-soul that we are individuals and members of one whole. And when you come to the Fourth, and more particularly to the Fifth stage, you will realise how fine and beautiful is this brotherhood within the one being; how it deepens and intensifies existence; how it destroys the cold selfishness so necessary to an earth life, where one living creature must continually destroy another's manifestation in matter in order to maintain its physical life.

In the Fourth stage the soul becomes sensitive of the group-soul, and through the awareness there arises a great change. He begins gropingly to realise the character of experience, the possibilities of mind; and in this Fourth stage if he is a Soul-man he is peculiarly liable to error. That is to say, once he becomes cognisant of the group-soul and of its many emotional and intellectual experiences he may, if a certain section of that group-soul be in a fixed mould, take upon himself its shape and remain within it for aeons of time. In this connection when I write "mould" I desire to indicate a certain special outlook. For instance, a fanatical Buddhist or a very devout Christian may be held within the groove of his earthly beliefs. For those other souls in his community are, perhaps, also, held in the chains of those particular ideas. So there he may remain, making no progress, in a thought or in a memory world which consists of the Christian or of the Buddhist dream. He is held fast in the tentacles of an octopus. This octopus is the earthly Christian or Buddhist idea of an Afterlife, their view of the universe as created when on earth.

Now, you will recognize that such conditions tend to inhibit progress. For it means—to use another metaphor—dwelling in an intellectual chrysalis, living in the past earthly conceptions. And it is needful that the journeying soul should come to a state in which he can at will survey them, but not be held by them, or be imprisoned in their limitations.

Spirit-man

Spirit-man is not caught in this eidolon or living ghost, in this wraith of earthly beliefs. The great masters are not thus ensnared. Christ, the

Son of God, entered into Hades, but He did not abide in any of the other planes of being. Christ, being inspired directly by God, was connected with no group-soul. He passed from Hades out Yonder; for His physical body was, during His lifetime on earth, the direct expression in the clay of that Essence, the Imagination of God. Truly, Christ was a limited expression of the Whole, was in earthly life linked to the Whole. But every Christian born upon the earth is inspired by some individualized spirit. When I write "individualized" I desire to indicate that it is a thought of God; it is not, therefore, the Whole, it is not the Fount of all life.

So there are numerous fanatical Christians who, though they led lives of rectitude on earth, committed certain intellectual sins. These might be summed up in the phrase "rigidity of thought," "an outlook limited by fanaticism." Briefly, they are wedded to a limited concept. in the fourth stage of existence they must learn how to escape from such a prison if they are to make further progress. these remarks apply equally to Buddhists, Mahommedans, and all those other fanatical adherents of various religions or, as in the modern world, of scientific conceptions. for science tends more and more to become a religion or special outlook for many human beings.

Now, if the soul is to pass from the Fourth to the Fifth stage he must first shake off, cast from him any dogma, any special earthly outlook which has shaped his mentality, which confines it; so that his vision is limited, and his experiences are, therefore, also limited; consciousness of reality being thus withheld from him.

Chapter 7

The Plane of Flame

The Fifth Plane

Birth into the Fifth Stage

There comes a time when the soul who dwells on the Fourth plane of life prepares for the incident of death. This death does not resemble the death of man. At this particular point in evolution the soul has perfect and absolute control of form, of his appearance, of his eidolon or living ghost. This is the last veil between him and a conception of existence without form. He must free himself before he can go up another rung of the ladder, and freedom can only come through the deliberate process called "The Breaking of the Image." It is the farewell to appearance, to form as a necessity, to colour, to feeling as a certainty, as a condition of life.

Again the soul enters into unconsciousness; and when he is born into the Fifth stage he has cast from him certain attributes that were his when he still inhabited the Image; for his soul was, in part, that Shape of Light he has now discarded.

Between each plane there is this lapse into apparent oblivion, a stilling of all processes, a great calm. It is called Hades by the ancients. Here the soul seems to pause. Slowly, however, vision returns, the traveller perceives, imaged upon the glimmering sea of eternity, all his experiences on previous planes; all the past images that make up the story of his life are spread before him. He studies them in the light of his Unifying Principle or spirit. They rouse, according to his nature, his varying desires, intellectual and emotional. He knows then that he must choose either to go forward or backwards. The spirit actually forces the choice. It has to be made according to the fullness of his experiences in the previous life. He has entire free will, but inevitably he chooses his greatest need. When at the gate of Illusionland, the Animal-man chooses to drop back into a physical existence. When at the gate of the many-coloured world, the Soul-man sometimes chooses to drop back into the first division of this region, which, in its last divisions, is the apotheosis of form.

However, supposing that his review of his previous lives is satisfactory, be will decide to go on to the Fifth stage, and then the great calm is broken. There arises a tempest wherein he discards his desire for existence in etherealised form, in that plane of colour. He discards then a certain part of himself which he will not lose but resume in the greater wholeness of the Sixth stage.

The Symbol of the Fifth Stage

It is necessary to describe by some symbol each chapter in the Book of Life. The term "flame" expresses the Fifth stage. For now the soul becomes emotionally whole, aware not alone of himself, but of all those other souls who are of his group. He remains himself, yet is all those other selves as well. He no longer dwells in form—as it is conceived by man—but he dwells still in what might be described as an "outline." All the past emotions, passions, intellectual modes of expression belonging to his companion souls shape this outline, an outline of emotional thought; a great fire which stirs and moves this mighty being now.

While he abides in this Fifth plane experience is manifold, is a multiplication, loses, in a sense, its apparent oneness. He lives indeed a life that seems to burn like a flame. It is a time of severe discipline, of vastly increased intellectual feeling, of great limitations, of boundless freedoms, of the glimpsing of infinite horizons. "Swoons of contemplation, agonies of dreaming," states in which all lucid thought lies fallow, states in which the intense feverish activities of all the passionate existence of his comrade souls flame through his being. He is thus all the time becoming more and more merged with the Unifying Spirit.

A rare intensity of feeling, of joy, of ecstasy, of sorrow, of dark despair nourish him, feed his life. Yet, all the while, he is, in a sense, apart, aloof. He is not caught in the storm of this emotional whirlpool. He is sensible of it, yet rides above it. His attitude, however, does not resemble that of St. Simeon Stylites, who remained upon his pillar remote and aloof from the gorgeous ancient world which was playing out its drama in those Mediterranean lands of his day.

The soul, on this Fifth level of consciousness, is continuously conscious. There are now no gaps, no periods of non-existence. He revels in the emotional and intellectual life of all those comrade souls who are on the various rungs of the ladders which reach up to the One Spirit and are lighted by it. But this soul, at the climax of his existence on the plane of flame, is as an artist who lives in his masterpiece, derives from it, in all its features, in the freshness of its evolving, changing creation, that strange exultation which may, perhaps, at one rare moment, be known to a creative genius—though very faintly—while he still lives upon the earth.

This state on the Fifth plane may be imagined but not understood or conceived by a man's mind. To the travelling soul the purpose of his existence will seem to be, at last, revealed. He tastes of Heaven and yet the revelation of the last mystery still tarries, still awaits the completion of the design of which he is a part.

It is a glorious existence, despite certain sinister aspects. The Soul-man, however, may not leave it for the Sixth plane until the group-soul is complete, until those other souls, necessary to this design woven in the tapestry of eternity, have also attained to this level of consciousness. Some may still be far behind. But while in this state of being, the Soul-man becomes aware of the emotional life of all the more primitive souls who inhabit denser and denser matter and, yet, belong to his group. He becomes aware, in short, of all the parts of the great body which his spirit, or the Unifying Principle, feeds with its Light. He realises the subconscious life of the flower, the insect, the bird, the beast, all those forms which are connected with the governor of his being, that Light from Above.

The Construction of the Group-soul

The actual construction of the group-soul must be clearly visualised. Its spirit feeds, with life and mental light, certain plants, trees, flowers, birds, insects, fish, beasts, men and women; representatives of living creatures in varying states of evolution. It inspires souls who are on various planes, various levels of consciousness in the After-death. It feeds, also, creatures on other planets. For the spirit must gather a harvest

35

of experience in every form. Gradually these intelligences evolve and merge. The experience necessary to the spirit is completed when all the souls necessary to the design have reached this Fifth plane. Once they become sensible of their oneness and their individuality they may go forward to the Sixth plane. There is, then, a breaking of the threads, a casting away of the dross of emotional experience, a sifting and changing on the part of all these souls. They pass once more into Hades and review, in that state, all that now lies behind them.

Chapter 8

The Plane of White Light

The Sixth Plane

Pure Reason

Light, though composed of many colours, is colourless. The spirit, though composed of many souls, is above and beyond pleasurable and painful moods of the mind. It belongs, therefore, to the Sixth plane, which is suitably described by the symbol of white light.

Now, on this level of consciousness pure reason reigns supreme. Emotion and passion, as known to men, are absent. White light represents the perfect equanimity of pure thought. Such equanimity becomes the possession of the souls who enter this last rich kingdom of experience. They bear with them the wisdom of form, the incalculable secret wisdom, gathered only through limitation, harvested from numberless years, garnered from lives passed in myriad forms. Knowledge of good and evil and of what lies beyond good and evil now belongs to them. They are lords of life, for they have conquered. They are capable of living now without form, of existing as white light, as the pure thought of their Creator. They have joined the Immortals.

The purpose of the Sixth plane of being might be described as "the assimilation of the many-in-one," the unifying of all those mind-units I have called souls, within the spirit. When this aim has been achieved, the spirit which contains this strange individualized life passes out Yonder and enters into the Mystery, thereby fulfilling the final purpose, the evolution of the Supreme Mind.

Chapter 9

Out Yonder, Timelessness

The Seventh Plane

Part of the Divine Principle

Again the choice must be made. Is the soul prepared to make the great leap, prepared to pass wholly from time into time-lessness, from an existence in form into formlessness? This is the most difficult of all questions to answer. Only a very few reply in the affirmative when first faced with it.

The Seventh state might be described as the "passage from form into formlessness." But pray do not misunderstand the term "form-lessness." I merely wish to indicate by it an existence that has no need to express itself in a shape, however tenuous, however fine. The soul who enters that Seventh state passes into the Beyond and becomes one with God.

This merging with the Idea, with the Great Source of spirit does not imply annihilation. You still exist as an individual. You are as a wave in the sea; and you have at last entered into Reality and cast from you all the illusions of appearances. But some intangible essence has been added to your spirit through its long habitation of matter, of ether the ancestor of matter, of what the scientists call empty space, though, if they but knew it, empty space is peopled with forms of an infinite fine-ness and variety.

Actually the passage from the Sixth to the Seventh state means the flight from the material universe, from that space which is a part of it. You dwell not only outside of time but outside of the universe on this last plane of being. Yet you can be and are, in one sense, within the universe. You as part of the Whole—and by the Whole I indicate God—may be likened to the sun; your rays pervade the material universe, yet your spirit remains detached from it, reigning in the great calm of eternity. To be of the universe and to be apart from it is, possibly, the final achievement, the goal of all endeavour.

In a few brief words I have spanned existence within aeons of time, and I have endeavoured to give you a glimpse of that mystery, timelessness. When you dwell out Yonder, you, as a part of the Divine Principle in its essence, are wholly aware of the imagination of God. So you are aware of every second in time, you are aware of the whole history of the earth from Alpha to Omega. Equally all planetary existence is yours. Everything created is contained within that imagination, and you, now by reason of your immortality, know it and hold, as the earth holds a seed, the whole of life, the past, the future, all that is, all that shall be forever and forever.

The Beyond baffles description. It is heart-breaking even to attempt to write of it.

That Spirit-man, God the Son, expressed a great truth when He said," Many are called and few are chosen." Only a very few pass out Yonder during the life of the earth. A certain number of souls attain to the sixth state, but remain in it or, in exceptional cases for a lofty purpose, descend again into matter. They are not strong enough to make the great leap into timelessness, they are not yet perfect.

Chapter 10

The Universe

The Buddhist maintains that the Universe is unreal. It is unreal only so long as you are caught in its web, governed by its laws, controlled by its matter or by that invisible substance I have called an air of matter.

The term "unreal" implies falsehood, sham, humbug. The soul, when he manifests himself in form, is limited by that form. He cannot know truth because he is imprisoned in that shape. He has, during his life on those first five planes, a limited view. Like a horse, wearing blinkers, he has a very poor idea of the world about him. The essential unreality arises through this specialized view merely of a piece of the road before him. Further, the form lies in the picture of this road which it conveys to the soul. So the Buddhist is in one sense right when he claims that the Universe is unreal.

But when the sage claims that the ultimate goal is one of extinction within Nirvana—extinction though not annihilation—he is using dangerous terms. He claims that we are extinguished once we reach this state of grace, this World of the Absolute. He suggests, however, that at any rate we are existing in unconditioned being; we are entirely apart from the Universe, freed from its essential unreality.

Actually, only on the Seventh plane when we are one with the Supreme Idea do we realise the reality of the Universe. It is unreal so long as it imprisons soul and spirit. It is real once these are merged and freed from it, dwelling in the infinite liberty of Pure Intelligence.

Once that state is attained we perceive that old masterpiece, the Universe, as a Whole. We realise it in every microscopic detail, and in its greatest proportions. We perceive the Whole of it as an intellectual concept within the Supreme Idea. We perceive the part of it that is playing out its drama. And thus we exist as the seer and the lover, experiencing all that life as an act of thought. So we reach the zenith of experience. We know the reality of the material Universe, we are aware of the other reality, the Idea, which contains its duplicate from the beginning to the end as a thought. We cannot be said to be extinct. We are one in the great harmony of Mind, we are individual in the love of the Creator for His creation which is contained within him, which is manifested in part.

We receive from all those myriad spirits who control parts of the material universe the complete impression of it in its least, in its greatest aspects. Therefore we live as never before, we are caught in no Nirvanic swoon. And we join in that contemplation of the destruction of the present Universe, of the creation, life and extinction of other universes, and so on endlessly. We live in the intellectual concept of them all and we are aware of that part which now plays out its drama on the stage of eternity.

Try to realise the dual character of existence when you think of the word "Universe"; then it may be easier to understand the nature of life.

There are physical atoms and there are psychic units. The psychic unit develops as it dwells within and without the physical atoms, in the various stages of existence. The psychic unit dwells within the fantasy of ever finer and finer substance, gaining all the while. The psychic unit escapes from that substance, returns to its home in the Idea. But this escape does not mean annihilation. It is one now and yet many, just as the physical atoms of the human body are one and yet many.

Understand, therefore, that the Universe is only unreal so long as you dwell within its confining web, within form. It is real when you are free from it and are able from Out Yonder to survey it as a whole and to know it as an act of pure thought.

Chapter 11

From the World of Eidos

The Plane of colour

The discarnate being who has conveyed this message has remained in touch with the earth and has followed, step by step, since his death at the beginning of the century, the progress of science, the Great War, which has been continued in the economic war. He has, through communion with the inner mind of his friends who still exist in physical bodies, perceived the change in man's spiritual outlook, perceived his urgent need for some cogent assurance of a spiritual world. Because a man dies, it does not follow that he loses touch with the earth, with that state of Penia—poverty—from which he rose into the delights of the plane named Illusion, from which he penetrated into the world of Eidos—pure form—to the human soul the Heaven World, the ultimate goal. For while on earth the human soul has, in rare moments, perceived that world but has not passed beyond it even when in the loftiest mystic trance.

We intelligences who have journeyed as far as Eidos may, when we choose, journey back to the state of Penia and commune with those who love us or who are to us mentally akin.

We perceive, then, the strange disorder of the world of men and women. We recognize the causes of that disorder and the purpose behind them. We realise the necessity for such disorder and at the same time we desire to convey some indication of the Great Reality.

For this reason I, Frederic Myers, have endeavoured to trace a rough outline of the road man must follow in the After-death if he be a seeker of immortality.

Chapter 12

The Incident of Death

To those of us who have reached that "unseen bourne" from which travellers in a changed aspect frequently return, death is an incident or a mere episode which we regard with a certain tenderness and not with any pain. To human beings, however, death should seem as a night at an inn, as a halt on the long road home.

It may be a night of feverish insomnia, or heavy with fear; a night full of strange dreams, or a period of almost undisturbed peace. Always there is, contained in it, a time of stillness, of sinking gloriously into rest. Nevertheless, the soul eventually wakens, to a new day. And, in dawn and dark alike, he is surrounded by certain of his discarnate kindred, by some of those who are woven into the pattern of his destiny.

Before we discuss death further we must be agreed on the meaning of one word which has caused much confusion of thought. The term "discarnate being" does not imply separation from any body whatsoever, but from exclusive association with the physical body. For, until the wayfarer reaches the Sixth plane, he must customarily use some form, some vehicle of expression, some outward sign or symbol of himself.

Many are these forms. For our present purpose it is advisable that I should name only four of them.

(1) The double or unifying body—in my opinion falsely named the astral body.
(2) The etheric body.

(3) The subtle body.

(4) The celestial body or shape of light.

The two latter are occupied by the soul on the higher planes and can be altered greatly in appearance by a mental act, or by an act of will.

Now, discarnate intelligences have probably informed you that the secret of death is to be found in the rate of speed at which the outer shell vibrates. For instance, a human being is primarily aware of the visible world about him because his body is travelling at its particular rate of speed. Alter the timing of your physical form, and the earth, men, women and all material objects, will vanish for you as you vanish for them. Death, therefore, means merely a change of speed. For the purpose of this change a temporary dislocation is necessary, for the soul must pass from one body travelling at a certain vibration to another travelling at a different rate or time.

This entry into the next life involves no sudden break, no leap, as it were, into new conditions. There must, necessarily, be an intermediate state. Even Christ entered into it, abiding, as you have been told, for a period in Hades.

And so we come to the first question. In what form does the human being express himself during the hours that immediately follow the moment when the physician declares that "life is extinct" "Where is the beloved?" we ask in our wordless misery as we watch by that shell, which, a few minutes previously, contained that bright, living personality; for us so radiant and so dear, quick in perception, eager in intelligence. During the hour after the passing of a soul with whom we have been intimately bound it is hard to believe in extinction. And ours is a right intuition when we instinctively refuse to believe that all is finished, that the soul has come to his journey's end.

During the whole of a man's earthly life he is accompanied by the double or unifying body. It is the link between the deeper mind and the brain, and has many important functions. When you fall asleep your consciousness no longer controls the physical shape. There is not only an apparent cutting off, but an entry into apparent oblivion. The usual disordered dreams are frequently but the play of nerves roused and irritated by the daily activities. Actually, during sleep, the soul exists within the double while the body is recharged with nervous energy, with life-units. So sleep has been wisely recognized as being even more important than food or drink.

46

Space does not permit further discussion of this aspect in the life of man. It is necessary only for you to realise that the double, if it could be made visible, is, in appearance, an exact counterpart of the physical shape. The two are bound together by many little threads, by two silver cords. One of these makes contact with the solar plexus, the other with the brain. They all may lengthen or extend during sleep or during half-sleep, for they have considerable elasticity. When a man slowly dies these threads and the two cords are gradually broken. Death occurs when these two principal communicating lines with brain and solar plexus are severed.

It is a well-known fact that life occasionally lingers in certain cells of the body after the soul has fled. This phenomenon has always baffled the physician, but there is a simple explanation for it. The double still adheres to the shell by means of certain of the threads which have not yet been broken. The soul does not suffer in the physical sense if thus delayed in his journey. He may suffer in the sense that he has, thereby, a greater awareness of the immediate surroundings of his physical body. It gives him the power to perceive his friends and relations wherever this worn-out garment lies. As a rule, however, he obtains complete freedom from earth's detaining grasp within an hour—or a few hours—of death.

When you watch by the dead or grieve for a departed friend, do not be anxious or concerned for him in the period immediately following his release. For the soul, at that time, is usually in a state of half-sleep. All the agony, all the strange dreams, the tortured fever of mind precede the translation of the soul to the double. At the moment of death—unless that death is of a violent character—peace reigns about the human consciousness. It is resting in dimness and sometimes is capable of perceiving those dear friends or relatives who have already passed to another life.

Conditions, of course, vary enormously. The man or woman who has never deeply loved or cared for any other human soul may, at death, rise from the body of clay into loneliness and into a night that, in its impenetrable blackness, is like no night on earth.

This state of complete isolation, however, is only allotted to a few human beings. The egoist or the cruel man will be condemned to it, but, for such a fate, his selfishness must be inordinate, his cruelty considerable.

The average man or woman when he or she is dying suffers no pain. They have become so dissevered already from the body that when the flesh seems to be in agony the actual soul merely feels very drowsy and has a sensation of drifting hither and thither, to and fro, like a bird resting on the wind.

This sensation has its own easeful delight after the pain of the illness which has led the soul to the change of death. So, grieve not for the apparent agony of the dying, rejoice because they are already freed from the torment, are already fluttering between two existences and abide in that nameless content which is due to the quiescence of mind and awareness.

Slowly the soul then rises into the double and for a brief time hovers above the physical counterpart. Some day men will be able to photograph this moment, and the being that passes thus may be registered on the plate as a little white cloud, a pale essence. Only so can this kernel of personality appear to even the finest material instrument. But, to discarnate beings, very different will seem the flight of the soul, for the perceptions of the etheric body are far more finely attuned. And usually those relatives or friends who attend upon death journey to it from the etheric world.

The Place of Shadows (Hades)

It is not possible to deal with even a tithe of the conditions which prevail in Hades for the multitude of the newly dead. I will, therefore, merely trace the course of an average man who has led a well-ordered life on earth.

According to the nature of the individual, so, also, is the length of his stay in the place of shadows. After a vision of the blood—kindred or psychic—kindred, and sometimes after communion with them, the soul rests seemingly within a veil, in a state of peaceful quiescence, of semi-suspended consciousness, seeing fragmentary happenings of his past life—these being now neither tainted by fear nor whipped by emotion. He watches this changing show as a man drowsily watches a shimmering sunny landscape on a midsummer day. He is detached and apart, judging the individual who participates in these experiences, judging his own self with the aid of the Light from Above.

The terms "Within the Husk" or "The Play of the Shadow Show" define this period. Souls vary considerably in their reactions to it. Some retain scarcely any recollection of it. Others are too aloof and too drugged by the condition of peaceful quiescence to feel either pleasure or pain. But all the while progress is being made, the etheric body is loosening, working out, withdrawing from the husk, until, at last, judgment is completed. The soul takes flight, casts the husk from him as a man throws an old cloak from off his shoulders. For the Spirit or Light from Above has accomplished its work of summing up, leaving to the traveller the final decision.

Once our pilgrim has, as it were, cast his skin, flung away the tattered remnant that bound him to mortality, he passes into the world of illusion and resumes full consciousness. The double, re-imaged within the veil, becomes the body of the man in the next life, only the outer rind or After-image has been flung away.

Three or four days of earth time may suffice for this experience of the Shadow Show, for the re-knitting and readjustment of the ego to the etheric body. It is true, however, that certain abnormal men and women linger a long while in Hades and wander to and fro in its grim ways, encountering certain strange beings who hover near the borders of the physical world, who wake old sorrows and troubles in the minds of men, and who play upon the understandings of certain individuals they would possess while still in the flesh, dethroning the reason, stealing from man his birthright. But these creatures have no part in the chronicle of death. For they cannot harm or hinder the pilgrims who journey from the world to us, drifting without pain or stress through Hades, that place of half-lights, of drowsy image-making, and, with a few exceptions, in no way or sense a place of fear or suffering.

Memory and Identity after Death

Physiologists will tell you that memory is merely a condition of the brain. Injure a certain part of that delicate organism and the healthy individual will become mentally a blank, will be quite unable to recall any fact concerning himself, any past experience whatsoever.

Actually, this unfortunate man has not forgotten his past nor is he intellectually a blank. A certain part of the mechanism of the brain has ceased to function, so he is unable to manifest any intelligence, dependent on memory, to the visible world of men. But he is still intellectually alive, and retains complete power over his memory apart from his actual physical body. For the double or unifying shape is the counterpart of that physical body, and registers, more or less as the brain registers, facts and experiences in the life of its owner.

Bear in mind that the double accompanies the man from birth till death, houses and shelters his soul, serves him even more faithfully than the actual physical shape of which he is daily aware.

According to the human view, memory is necessary to a sense of identity, to the idea of individuality and all that is conveyed by the words "soul" or "consciousness." Sense of identity, however, is not lost through the change of death, for the soul finds his fundamental memory-centre in his double which, as I have informed you, is his habitation in the Afterlife.

As the double* casts away an outer husk, only its essential part, the etheric body, which has accompanied the traveller and functioned for him all through his earth life, goes on and serves the soul on the plane of illusion, maintaining continuity of individuality through continuity of memory.

During the play of the shadow show this etheric shape gathers new force, is remoulded, readjusted to the soul, and there is a strange and wonderful renewal, a sense of flooding life in the last stages as the butterfly breaks through the chrysalis, as the individual who has entered the period within the husk—an old decrepit man in appearance—passes from it in a youthful body, pulsating with life and eager with human desires.

On the plane of illusion these desires are satisfied.
"We shall not all sleep"

Apart from Revelations, what is the teaching of the Bible concerning the Afterlife? "We shall not all sleep, but we shall all be changed." The words of St. Paul harmonise with the account of the Afterlife given in these pages. The phrase "we shall not all sleep" implies that many do sleep until "the last trumpet sounds," until the end of the earth. In what garden, in what world, in what space do these sleepers rest?

---

* If I recollect rightly, certain Easterns believe that the human being, in his construction, resembles an onion and possesses at least six bodies which all exist at the same time. I have found no evidence of these numerous shapes. They may, of course, exist. I can only write out of my own knowledge.—F. W. H. M.

As birds live in air so do these souls exist in the etheric zone which is about the earth. They are inhabitants of the world of illusion. Now, on that plane, save in the last stages, there is an almost entire absence of conflict and effort, accordingly there is an absence of any true creation. Many human beings regard such a state as the most desirable condition of being. When they ask for heaven while on earth they indicate, by the word "heaven," a life without conflict or effort. Those of them who are satisfied with such a life meet it after death in the illusion world, and so linger within its borders until "the last trumpet sounds." This phrase of St. Paul's must be read symbolically. It possessed its own peculiar meaning in the ancient world, a meaning which has been lost. The souls who rest on the Third plane until they are roused by this summons may be fitly called "the sleepers." For what does sleep indicate if not an absence of conscious conflict and effort?

Existence seems in many respects as real to the occupant of the world of illusion as it does to king, politician, lawyer, doctor, clergyman and working man on earth. But it contains one important difference. The soul has no need to put forth struggle or effort. He obtains his desire through the mere act of desire. So he cannot be said to live as he did on earth, or gloriously as he will live in the world of Eidos. He is, in truth, the sleeper mentioned in the New Testament.

"We shall not all sleep, but we shall all be changed." This text infers that some of the dead do not sleep. In other words, many of those, who have died, scorn the pleasant fields of illusion, their deep content; they desire conflict, creation, effort, and so they either become incarnate again or they wisely choose to go upwards and to enter the world of Eidos, to find, indeed, life more abundantly within that masterpiece. For in that state of grace the traveller meets with the finest glories of appearance, with the triumph of life in form.

The After-image, or Husk

The After-image might be likened to an old traveller's cloak. Though he discards it, it remains by the roadside and may be picked up and worn again.

Ghosts have been known to walk for many years in certain old mansions at certain seasons, or inconsequently, without apparent rhyme or reason. Say to yourself if you meet one of these restless shades: "Here walks the ancient cloak, the old disguise, perhaps, of some Roundhead or Cavalier, of some cowled monk or holy nun, of some modern gentle-man who has indulged in butchery or has himself been murdered—with new weapons but with the same old passions of rage and hate behind him."

It is that same repetitive passion that provides the energy which, for a brief space, re-animates the Afterimage. But it may not walk in its own place if there be not association of memory, an energising thought or idea behind it. Somewhere within the far realms of space exists the brawler who died so violently, or the nun or monk who enriched that cloak with all their brooding religious passion. They are resting, with-drawing temporarily from their active life in another sphere, and, for a moment, by reason of the binding threads of past fate, envisage again the old scene where they lived or from which they took their leave of life. They cast on it but the careless thought which is now unclouded by remorse, regret or any emotion. But the mere light flick of their thought stirs up the old cloak, causing it to masquerade again within the build-ing or about the grounds which were familiar to it in life.

But be assured that the essential ego does not return and play the old part, making mockery of it on the stage of earth, with its insub-stantial vapouring, with its elusive vanishing into air. No; such ghosts or phantoms, who wander thus meaninglessly, are indeed but ancient garments tossed back to visibility at the appointed hour when the man or woman who has "inner" sight is present to record this decep-tive masquerade.

All rules have their exceptions and so all hauntings may not come under any one rule. But it is accurate to accept the average ghost as a per-sistence of a manifestation of energy through the medium of the After-image, focused by the pull of an old thread of passionate memory.

Violent Death

Sometimes the dead do not know that they are dead. This statement may seem incredible. Yet it is true in certain fairly rare cases.

Only the past history of the dead man can make clear this curi-ous lack of apprehension of his state. If he passes through the gates of death bearing with him a passionate love of material possessions, he will, even after a fleeting glimpse of his discarnate kindred, tenaciously hold to the belief that he is still a man of flesh and blood, wandering, perhaps, on the hills in a mist, but still filled with the life of earth. He will passionately seek for his house, his money, or whatever is his particular treasure, in the dark ways beyond death. And sometimes they may appear in an elusive manner a little ahead of him, leaping thus only for a brief moment before his subjective vision and then vanishing, the cloud descending once more, reducing all things for him to nullity again. Such an egoist will linger for some time on the borders between the two worlds, freedom coming when the force of that passion for material possessions weakens and fades.

There are also certain others who linger thus in Hades, but not unhappily as a rule. I refer to certain young men of careless, animal and, occasionally, vicious life who die violent deaths. These poor fellows are suddenly wrenched from their bodies while still they are in the prime of manhood. They are not, in any sense, capable of grasping, for a while, the difference between earth life and the Afterlife. So they too remain in ignorance, and must remain in a kind of coma until the delicate etheric body has recovered from the shock of a too rapid severance from the earthly shape.

However, the great majority of men and women after death flit like passenger-birds through Hades, resting only for a brief while here or there, making one contact with their old friends or relatives who preceded them, held but for a short spell by the play of the shadow show and then loosed into the new life, into the effortless land where the pattern is again woven, but on that plane it will have no new design, no new threads or colours.

The Death that follows a Period of Senility

The very old may, before their passing from earth, in part lose memory or lose their grasp of facts, their power of understanding. This tragic decay all too often causes the observer of it to lose his faith in an Afterlife. For the soul seems, under such circumstances, merely the brain This, however, is a false conclusion. The soul, or active ego, has been compelled partially to retire into the double during waking hours because the cord between the brain and its etheric counterpart has either been frayed, or has snapped. The actual life of the physical body is still maintained through the second cord and through any of those threads which still adhere to the two shapes. So the aged, apparently mindless man or woman, is in no sense mindless. He or she has merely withdrawn a little way from you and has no need of your pity, for, through that withdrawal, his awareness is almost wholly confined within his unifying body—the body of his resurrection.

The Pattern

Beyond ambition, beyond any human forms of selfishness, beyond the struggling, scarcely leashed desires, are affection, love, the drawing, intangible force between kindred souls. It is stronger than death, it conquers despair and may conquer on all the finite levels of existence. It must be reckoned as a cosmic principle and is known as "the power behind the pattern" which is being woven for you as long as time, for you, exists.

Death seems terrible to the average man because of its apparent loneliness. If he but knew it, his fears are vain; his dread of being reft from the pattern—that is to say, from those he loves—has no foundation, has no real substance behind it. For, wherever he may journey after death, always will he be caught again into the design of which he is a part, always will he find again, however deep his temporary oblivion or however varied his experience, certain human souls who were knit into his earth life, who were loved deeply, if sometimes blindly or evilly, by him in those bygone days.

It is true that the more primitive types are incapable of the love of the whole being. They fail to understand that to love in this manner is to observe the first law of progress; for it is a love that has within it the seeds of immortality. Such primitive souls as are at the beginning of the pattern frequently initiate its design with hatreds, deathless antagonisms, which, encountered again on the Third plane, hound back such souls to earth, where they are re-born, and where, if progress is made, they may learn the first spiritual law, namely, the Law of the Beloved.

No man or woman who has mastered it need fear death, for, even if he go first, some other who is in his pattern—and therefore truly his kindred—will speedily join him, give him greeting in the Great Adventure which lies beyond death.

Call death your friend, hail death as your deliverer. For the darkness and soil which is in every earth love passes, vanishes with your passing.

Chapter 13

The Evolution of the Psyche

In the previous pages will be found a rough chart of existence. It was inadvisable to enter, in such a chart, upon any detailed description of the qualities essential to the navigator if he would speedily and successfully steer his course across these strange worlds.

When I was on earth I was a firm believer in the power and strength of agape or love. In the New Testament St. Paul uses the word which is translated as "charity," but attributed to it a meaning which has been also allotted to love.

Here, in the afterlife, I perceive that neither of these words conveys the whole significance of the Good, for they have been so long interpreted by human and finite minds that they have become worn and defaced, soiled and obscured by contact with many natures of an infinitely varied character.

To some, the word "love" means only the passion which lights up between man and woman, to others, it is the intellectual love shared by two friends, kindred souls. Thirdly, and lastly, love is held by many to be compassion for others and to contain within it that communal sense of the brotherhood of man, that love, in a general sense, which has led, undoubtedly, to fine endeavour in past times.

But always these conceptions fall short of the ideal. Though again and again agnostic and Christian study the Gospels, image in their hearts the Sermon on the Mount, still they fail, still their understanding perishes in the presence of the great words of immortality.

No man or woman has ever really succeeded in understanding or grasping the whole lofty vision of love as it was seen by the Christ. So now, as I survey the present earth and perceive the chronicle of the years, I am sensible of the need of a word which has not been debased by men, which can still suggest and contain the primary need of the soul, which will define that urge so essential to the psyche when it would climb from one rung to another on the ladder of consciousness.

The permanent reality of progress is to be found in increase of wisdom. For wisdom may be defined as "right judgment concerning truth."

Upon every plane of being the conception of truth must necessarily be limited or enlarged by the conditions of life, by the form the soul assumes, or by that extension of consciousness which, at the last, tends to shake off form, as the trees in autumn cast off their leaves.

On the dense plane of matter known as earth the term "truth" is still holy and, to the minds of many men, unsoiled. It may, therefore, be used to illustrate what I believe to have been Christ's meaning where the word "love" is put into His mouth in the Gospels. But it is not complete unless "right judgment" is added to it.

Consider, then, the significance of "wisdom." For, clearly, within that lofty word resides the highest love between man and woman, intellectual love, compassion, faith and last, but not least, the power of vision. All these are possessed by the man or woman who rightly judges truth. And, on whatever plane your soul or the soul of the beloved is evolving, be assured that wisdom is the primary urge which causes this soul to choose to go up rather than down, to select the finer life, the greater reality, rather than existence in denser form, in more material worlds.

"Love your enemies. Bless them that persecute you." These beautiful and enigmatic phrases have troubled and perplexed every sincere Christian who has endeavoured to apply them to his own life. Only through wisdom can he, in any measure, fulfill their command, expressing them literally in act and thought. For they are contained in wisdom. Their idea depends for its manifestation, for its very life, on right judgment of the truth.

The simple peasant, the humble working man or woman, ignorant in the eyes of the world, may yet be wholly wise if they possess this spiritual discernment, which, for the human soul, expresses Christ's vision when He spoke of "love."

So must it be on each plane of being in the Unseen. Wisdom is the light that, in every instance, gives shape and life to love, is its secret hidden root, is the inspiration, the power that causes the forward and upward progression expressed in the term—the evolution of the psyche.

PART TWO

INSTRUCTION ABOUT VARIOUS HUMAN FACULTIES AND OTHER MATTERS

Chapter 14

Free Will

The term "free will" presents different meanings to different people. For some it implies the idea that in all we do we are following out our own particular fancy or desire so far as is possible. For others, free will seems to imply simply the right to choose, the right, when we come to cross roads, to follow the particular lane that seems, from our point of view, the most alluring.

Perhaps we decided to travel along the beech-shaded road and not the road that is open on every side. Who makes that decision? I should call it the aggregation defined by the term, body, soul, and spirit. Now, all these are built up out of various elements, but all are one creation. They have been slowly shaped through the ages. All the hereditary influences must be included. All the influences of a psychic and a spiritual character are there. These seem innumerable to our finite minds. Circumstances, friends, enemies, relations, all help to mould that inner being which makes the decision to follow that beech-shaded road. Does it not strike you, therefore, that you are asking what is impossible because of the very nature of our being when you make the demand that free will must rule? We are obviously merely the creation of many other men and women living and dead. Therefore we are largely the victims of their varying influences and are bound to follow those tendencies implanted in us. In other words all mankind is, in a sense, one, and yet many. Man's history, his character since the dawn of the world, might be conceived as a vast web ever growing and growing, and the source of it all is to be found in the Master Spinner who is responsible for every particle of that fine fabric, for the whole history, the whole character of man since the beginning of time.

Now, you must realise that as God is the Creator, the Great Master Builder, He knows what shape the life of the individual will take before that individual is born. He knows exactly the nature of the unborn babe, how he will develop from the hour he leaves his mother's womb, where his tendencies will lead him, the manner in which circumstances will mould him. For the great picture of all creation has been conceived in the imagination of God before ever the babe has evolved out of what we call the void. For instance, the future of the earth is imaged already in the imagination of God. It has happened because He has already thought it. But what has not happened is the change in the individual soul, the manner, for instance, in which it reacts to the trials and the joys of life. The reactions of the soul are all that matter in connection with your earth life. Will sorrow embitter you? Will ruin but nerve you to fresh effort? In the latter instance, you create within yourself in that you increase the power of your will, increase your courage. Or will you give up hope and sink into penury, thus increasing the weakness of your character? You have, in short, free will only in the sense of creation, only in the moulding of your own soul. Now that is the important and vital factor in connection with your life on earth. For when you go back to the group-soul of which you are one, according to the mould of your soul so shall be the mould of circumstance in the future life of the young soul of your group who is about to be born. It is hard to put my idea into words.

God watches over the cosmic life of the group-souls. And, according to their growth, He plans or designs the future of the life of mankind. But because it was all imaged by Him at the beginning so is there little to change in the vast cosmic picture that lies in His imagination.

Chapter 15

Memory

Within and Without the Body

I shall try to give you a brief account of some of the aspects of memory as they present themselves to me. First of all, you would probably like to understand memory, as it is in the case of the living. What do you do? Your will decides that you shall remember the name of Tom Jones. It makes the effort to concentrate upon that image. What is the exact process? It draws to it a certain very fine essence invisible to the human eye. Scientists might describe that essence as something far subtler than electricity and yet of the same nature. This, if the will be strong enough, can be led to make the necessary imprint again upon what would appear to you, if you had the perception, to be something fluid, something that flows. This fluid penetrates matter, and, with the assistance of the essence I speak of, can become so shaped that it is able to get in touch with the cell in the brain that is ready to respond. The will, with the assistance of these two elements, is able to join as by a thread the image, Tom Jones, to the cell. You have such perverted ideas of space, as long as you are in matter, that you cannot for a moment grasp how millions of little images made in this manner are all in touch with the millions of cells in the brain through these threads. Imagine an immense spider's web about you. All the strands bear memories or thoughts to the brain as the wires transmit telegraphic messages, and can carry to the brain messages, or, rather, the sign of the image that has been created through impress being made on something plastic with the assistance of this essence.

Your words make it impossible. You have no term, for instance, for this clay that receives the impression. I call it clay, but it is not of the nature of matter. This clay—as I call it for want of a better word—is the substance out of which thought is constructed. Of course, it is not substance as you understand it. Very well, then, this clay receives all the impressions your sight, hearing, and touch convey, but it does not make the connecting thread with the brain cell unless your will makes the conscious effort which is necessary for its construction. You now ask: what is will? Will is the energy that flows to you from the large individual mind without you, added, of course, to the collection of images that are all attached to the physical brain as I have already tried to indicate. The will is influenced by the physical body. The larger mind contains that infinite subtlety of atoms that are not destroyed through the death of that crude machine, the body. Actually, though I call them atoms, they would appear to you to be of a fluid character. I want you to realise, though, that the essential You is something that is composite as long as you are alive. It is an alliance between what is material and what you call immaterial. The body or matter has certain yearnings brought about by the actual nature of its construction. These are not you, but they dominate you, because they can usually command much of what is immaterial and can enter into the directive process that goes on in the cells of the brain. These cells are so highly sensitive that they can and do respond to the stimulus of a being who is motion rather than substance. Think of your will, then, as motion; ever by its active energy coalescing these images—marshalling them—causing the brain, which is the only part at all sensitive to pure motion, to draw upon the threads that are attached to these images when the need for their uprisal in the consciousness is made manifest. I have tried to explain what you cannot possibly conceive so long as you are in matter.

Memory

Memory out of the body is a different affair altogether. When we become discarnate beings we are far more detached from the earthly images for the reason that they are no longer bound to us by matter through the medium of the brain cells. The threads, as you must realise, are broken by death. It does not mean that these images of all the impressions ever made on you are destroyed, they still exist, but we, when we choose, can, under certain psychic conditions, draw those images we desire to us by making the effort of the will that places us amongst them. We do not draw them to us as when we are alive, with labour and difficulty, we simply make the necessary effort which places us in the state that makes it possible for us to perceive the images we desire. Now, we are not in that state when we communicate through you. That is our difficulty. We are quite detached from these images, and unless the medium has the psychic power of absorbing the facts demanded from our memory—with our assistance, of course—we cannot provide you with the evidence you require. The ordinary human being does not possess this particular power, which is a kind of overflow of the fluid which takes the shape of your body and is about you, though invisible.

These images are outside the brain. They are outside the body, being connected by threads that are invisible to you because they pass through matter and are not themselves matter. They are amenable to touch certainly, but are not remembered unless a very considerable effort is made to draw in the appropriate thread and its image. Even then there are many images that cannot be drawn within the normal consciousness. I cannot find in the English language words sufficiently exact to make my meaning clear.

Now, memory may be likened to the sea. It is all about you, and as elusive as the water of the ocean. When we are alive we come to it like children with our small buckets and fill them with the salt fluid. How little we carry away up the sands. How easily and swiftly we spill it upon the ground. Yet, behind us is that vast area of water booming endlessly upon the shore. The sound of memory is now to me like the sound of the tide, as when in the olden days I listened to it through the summer evenings.

I want you to think of memory as this great sea. It gives of itself to the earth through all the seasons. It is, therefore, all about you as moisture is about you. Even when you are on earth you may draw from this invisible memory almost unknowingly. And, as one country has a damper atmosphere, a heavier rainfall than another, so will one mentality draw to it a greater share of the collective memory than another. It is changed when filtered through the brain of man; it takes upon itself his colour, his personality, and eventually it comes up to his consciousness as original thought, but horribly dull and unoriginal at times. For the average man draws through him mostly the recent memory ejected by many living brains. The thinker has a greater capacity for drawing to him the memories that lie in the depths of human nature, the strong memory, not the superficial one that is tossed off by the brain of man at the moment. What is rapidly cast off does not continue to live for any length of time. It is only the emotional memories, or the memories created by a fine vehemence, that permanently continue.

Man is like a power station, constantly generating the fresh electric fluid of memory, constantly receiving, constantly giving out again. Human beings cling to their individualities; probably it is but fitting that they should do so. But only what is fundamentally themselves, what is the very kernel of their being, survives the continual dissolution. For, my friend, in life we are mentally perpetually dying; in other words, as in every third season the tree casts off its leaves, so do we, as the years go trooping by, continually cast off our memories. And in so doing we change very considerably. What a stranger the boy Tom Jones of ten years old is to the man Tom Jones whose sixty years have sounded! How shy and self-conscious they would be if they met! How, in many respects, they would dislike each other! But, from far down, there would come some elusive stirring, some strange thrilling, deep calling to deep, if you will; so that these two, the boy aged ten and the man aged sixty, would, despite their superficial differences, be drawn to each other as surely as the magnet draws the iron. They would scarcely know why they thus responded, flew together despite their conscious incongruities. But they would inevitably respond, be thus drawn together. For something deeper than individual memory compels this unity. They share very few concrete memories, they are strangers. But the fine core of things has moved them to be comrades, friends.*

In like manner, when men and women journey into this new state of life they meet, perhaps after many years, wives, husbands, sons, daughters who have tarried twenty or thirty years behind them on the earth. If all is well, if they meet again in the world of the departed souls, they will not recognize each other through memory of facts. They will know each other through something that goes far deeper than that memory. Love and hate, caution and impetuosity, all the qualities that lie at the base of a man's or a woman's nature, will cause them to recognize each other, so that there is no need for reference, or for search in the *Book of Life*. The fundamental knowledge still remains, and the old ties may be renewed, that is, if they belong to the fundamental part of you. But

---

* The statements concerning discarnate beings contained in these two essays on memory apply to souls when they are living consciously on the Fourth plane. —F. W. H. M.

please believe me, since I died I have not remained stationary. I have been changing, evolving, putting on, if you will, like the trees, a fresh coat of leaves, but unchanged within; so that my wife and my children will know me though some of my earth memories be buried as the foliage underground when winter comes.

In stating that some of my earth memories are a closed book to me I do not wish to indicate that they are cut off irretrievably from me. They do not, in my present state, assist me, for I am exceedingly occupied on the Fourth plane in forging new impressions out of a fresh set of experiences in form. Be assured I shall, in the intermediate state between the Fourth and Fifth plane of being, review all those earth memories again.

Chapter 16

The Great Memory

The Great Memory is, if you will, the subconscious mind of the whole human race. In our life, as in yours, there is the consciousness, the self known to other discarnate beings who live in the same state as those akin to them fundamentally. But there is also a deeper self, which is the self of the world, imperishable as I believe, containing what was and is, containing also what shall be. For the history of man from the earliest to the latest times is all within what is sometimes called "The Tree of Memory." You may say, "But future events have not yet happened, so how can they have shaped themselves upon the ether?" I tell you they have happened, for they have already been born in the imagination of God. But the future is difficult to read, I mean difficult for men to read, because the memory of the future has not been so deeply impressed upon the invisible timeless substance, in that it has been thought only once and not twice, thought by the Maker of the Universes: therefore, it is very fine and faint, and only its echo is caught by certain mortals who have the inner hearing. Whereas the gross and clumsy subjective thinking of man causes past memories to be, from the point of view of the sensitive, more definitely shaped in the flowing energy.

I want you to understand the significance of this vast memory in the lives of the ever-living, whom you may call "departed souls." These, in pursuing their present existence, can live away from the memory of all past existence, or they can resume a vanished personality by picking up the threads from the Great Memory and sucking in from them, as you might suck a sugar cane, the nourishment of a past personality. It is not always perfectly shaped when the discarnate being endeavours to communicate. Sometimes only a little of the past individual's garment of mortality is taken from the great storehouse and, for a brief while, displayed.

Now I would call your attention to an important point in this connection. We, you and I, are each recorded on some page in this Great Memory. We must, as players in a drama, re-learn the old part before we endeavour to speak to our friends on earth, through a medium. As a rule we neglect this task, or we succeed in obtaining only a glimpse of the memory that enshrines our vanished personality. We have vanished and we have not vanished. It is hard to explain this duality. Fundamentally we are the same as we were when a loved wife, mother, or sister bade us "goodbye" in the earth life. We are the same in the sense that we should continue to have a feeling of repulsion for certain things and people we disliked on earth, and the old affections would flame up if we met again those people and things that were dear to us. But if by personality you mean the sum total of our earth memories—our knowledge of Greek and Latin, our knowledge of concrete facts—then we are indeed changed, in that we can, as a rule, only resuscitate the old knowledge by obtaining contact with that part of the Great Memory which is ours. Yet we do retain—apart from it—our old mentality, much of its idiosyncrasies. That part of ourselves that is no longer integral, that has become detached, is the fleeting physical consciousness of that period when we bade the earth farewell; is the aggregation of memory concerning facts in our earth life, concerning certain concrete knowledge memorised by us. Emotional memory remains an integral part of the soul, for it comes from the creative Life.

Chapter 17

Attention

For the Incarnate
and Discarnate Being

I will define attention. As you know it, in physiological terms attention is the direction by the will of a certain nerve-force into certain special cells of the brain. That is, suppose I want to recall the image of St. Mark's in Venice; I direct the nerve-force into that special cell or cells connected with my memory of Venice. The entity created by Venetian experiences wakes into life, and becomes for a time a "personality," while all the time, quite behind it, in the background, is the controlling will; but the Venetian self is expressing its personality during that period. I merely take Venice as an example. These centres of personality have been, I think, created usually by a network of far more complicated associations and memories. They have each of them been derived from a series of fundamental experiences that have cut deep into the soft material of the soul.

Attention for the Discarnate Being

Try and think of the mind as a web: in it are numerous centres about which radiate thoughts and memories. Any one of these centres can direct its attention towards the earth. We are all fundamentally one, but when we concentrate upon some special operation of thought we become divided. In order that we may become one again we have to travel far from you. We must be fused in the spirit again. I do not, by

71

the word "far," wish to indicate distance as you know it, I merely wish to indicate that the very fineness of our composition leads us, when we are one, to be remote from you. You possibly will not believe me when I tell you that each star has its own personality. It is one and yet it is many. In the same way you, even when in the body, are, in the same material sense, one yet many. There are myriads of little entities within you but there is only one mind or one channel for the mind. The interesting feature of my state here is that I am within a larger mind which is not a collective one but is rounded off from many others. Many of my affinities are contained in it. All those phases in my earth life are represented by these various centres.

I have spoken to you of attention in a physiological sense. I have described it as a stream of nervous energy, being directed towards certain cells or a certain cell in the brain, these being connected with certain images. Very well. As we are now constituted we have no material brain, but we possess a certain psychic web. This web is not exactly on the plan of the brain. It does not contain millions of tiny neurons or compartments, but it contains several centres which can draw or attract a stream of psychic energy from the Unifying Principle. If a great effort is made there can be attention in more than one direction, but not always. It is possible when we are communicating with the world that we can only supply one centre or focus at a time with this active stream or motive force. This is quite easy to understand, for a considerable effort of concentration is required when we manipulate another deeper mind. Sometimes we succeed in communicating with two people at once, but it is exceedingly difficult. The interesting point for you in connection with these centres or half-way houses is that the memory of what we have communicated is lodged therein, or rather it is in touch with that centre and no other centre with that focus, and also with the Unifying Principle, which, as you know contains many in one.

Chapter 18

The Subliminal Self

I promised to speak to you about the inner content of mind. I think, perhaps, I had better commence by speaking of man as a living organism. That seems a curious idea to me now, but I must use your terms as you understand them. To begin with, scientists have not in the least realised how very detached consciousness—or the soul—is from the body. The latter is the inheritance received from many past generations. It is in itself an empire, polyzoic and even polypsychic. It is, in fact, infinitely more complicated, with three degrees of nerves, those of the higher centres, those of the middle and lower. These nerves are the keys upon which our consciousness plays. Now, I want you to understand that we, in our etheric condition, to a certain degree correspond with the physical organism. Have you ever pondered over that mysterious phrase, "in the beginning the image was made flesh"? I may quote incorrectly, but that phrase, or one that is similar to it, which you will find in the Bible (John 1:14) contains a vast truth. The living organism is, to a certain degree, a reflection of what is in the Unseen. There is a Unifying Principle of which I have already told you. There are also minor consciousnesses which I have already spoken of as centres, or as the focus. When I communicate with the earth, one of these minor consciousnesses, or psychic entities, takes possession of the medium, supplanting one of the psychic entities which she possesses. We never supplant what I call the Unifying Principle in her; if we did, she would go mad. It is a very difficult feat, and is only attempted by certain malevolent entities on this side. Now, can you imagine a country, take England for example, dotted over with towns all self-contained, yet looking to that vast city London for general directions and for a certain essential stimulus? Such is the condition of the discarnate being. He is a kingdom, bounded by what would seem to have the appearance of a veil. It has a curious elasticity. I mean, we differ from the kingdom to which I have alluded in that we can alter at will the shape of this very subtle material or fluid. We differ in many other respects. Our surroundings are of a metetheric character. You may ask me to define this. It is exceedingly difficult. But I think I may say that it contains atoms of the very finest kind. They pass through your coarser matter. They belong to another state altogether.

You may then ask: "How does your world or state differ from our earth?" It differs very considerably, for the reason that this fluid is quite unformed. After death, if we are sufficiently developed, we enter into our subliminal self. When we were alive we believed that there were two forms of consciousness: one the inner mind, the other the supraliminal, that which was above the threshold, that which controlled our ordinary business, that which appeared to direct operations generally. We looked on the subliminal as being that which was below the threshold, the inner mind, the inspired part of our nature, the creative source. Very well then, since I have passed over I have come to realise that actually, in the sense of pure mind, there is no supraliminal part. There is in its stead an infinitely complicated machine which has become more and more subtilised through the centuries, so that now it responds to the slightest of vibrations, sent out by the subliminal, or what you may perhaps call the subconscious, mind. Of what, then, does the supraliminal or ordinary consciousness consist? Of a very wonderful nerve-memory; of all the physical desires of the body, to a large extent controlled by that nerve-memory; and lastly, and most important, of the reflection of the subliminal part of you. Usually, the subliminal sends its reflection, which, to a faint or a powerful degree, is received by the fluid shape which I call the nerve-memory. This, in its turn, transmits the reflection in vibrations to the brain. Normal consciousness is to a certain degree threefold. It consists in the main of the image interpreted by the nerve-memory, and of the material part, the brain, which is responsive to the image sent by this inner mind. But that is not by any means all. The brain and body, as a rule, must set the desire for the image in motion before the latter can be despatched and made perceptible. In short, the body must be receptive, or, rather, the nerves and brain must receive and register. These two alter and elaborate, or they simplify and give colour to, the contribution that has come from the higher portion of man's nature. There is also a reverse process: the assimilation of impressions of the material world by the brain which are transferred to the higher centres and returned in due course. There is, in short, a constant trafficking during the individual's waking hours between these various parts of his being.

Many points still require elucidation. You probably desire to know where is that positive, and very frequently objectionable, entity the "ego." It is a sum in arithmetic, a figure worthy of the attention of mathematicians. It is really the sum total of the physical needs of man, and the accretions through many generations of inherited memories, added to his innate capacity for corresponding with the inner mind and for receiving its image. Now there are times of creative activity which scholars have been kind enough to allocate to the inner mind. Then great works are produced, and you cannot understand the mystery of their creation. They are produced through a certain singular aptitude on the part of the brain, which responds to the message from the inner mind directing the nerve-memory. The fluid shape does not act as a medium, and there is in consequence no blurred interpretation. Added to this, of course, must be a considerable store of knowledge, or images, all connected with the brain-cells by those invisible threads of which I have already spoken. You must realise that the act of creation, then, is collaboration. The stream of energy from the inner mind moulds the work of art, partly out of these associations, these memories, but also partly out of the harvest of floating thoughts, from which it can draw more directly when the fluid shape is not the actual medium. In the case of the normal consciousness the fluid shape plays an important part and is largely the "ego." It will very frequently draw from the psychic entities, the minor consciousnesses; but these usually are directly bound up with the Unifying Principle, they are merely its tributaries. When there is a disintegration of personality it is sometimes due to one of these entities losing touch with the Unifying Principle, owing to the possible misbehavior of the fluid shape or nerve-memory, which sends out a too powerful appeal to this psychic entity. The central consciousness, however, is usually, if directly evoked, able to obtain control again. I want you, in the light of my remarks, to consider and study the evolution of man. The larger mind has been there, in a state at times unformed, from the dark ages, from the beginning if there ever was a beginning, which I doubt. At first this mind found it could only at times send faint reflections to primitive people, whom it had gradually evolved, created as a sculptor creates. But in time the form of man developed, and was the more easily able to receive the image. The Word was made flesh with greater and greater facility.

You may ask, in connection with mind, why it thus sought to express itself? It desired individuality; it, too, desired form; and form and individuality were, to a certain degree, achieved through this constant interchange between mind and matter. But, mark you, it is still the essence of matter—the nerves and nerve-memory—that dominates and controls the actions of the human being. So seek for the normal ego, when you are a living woman, in the nerve-soul, in the construction of the brain and body, and in the image sent by the Unifying Principle. The Word was made flesh. In that phrase you may find the whole mystery of man's nature, the sum total of his being.

You desire to know what is ordinary consciousness. The actual constructive force is, in its essence, the nerve-soul; but ordinary consciousness is a sum in arithmetic. The needs of the body, the cravings of the mechanisms, are all influencing the nerve-soul in its decisions. What you call the subconscious is the reflection, the light from above. Sometimes it is feeble because the summons is weak. It also plays a part in the decision. Time, of course, is a factor that puzzles you in this connection, but the whole organization is through centuries of evolution, so subtilised that it can make its decision rapidly. In the days of primitive man, the I, the constructive force—the "ego"—was principally the body; the nerves—the fluid shape even—were subordinate. I want you to understand that there are not, save in very rare cases, two wills making decisions at the same time consciously. There is only one, because there is only one channel; but the subliminal self, which is outside the larger mind—if you prefer that term—is exceedingly active, and, when messages in daytime are sent to it through the channel, that is to say, via the nerve-soul, then this mind works upon the message and sends it during sleep, in a new guise, back to the nerve-soul, which it can easily do, because the soul is apart from the body, quite still, and yet able to reflect the desired image which it craved for in waking hours. This is, on waking, attached by it to the brain cells, and you find some problem solved for you as by a magician when you are roused again out of sleep.

Initiative during the day, then, comes from the nerve-soul, fed by the image or the reflection from the subliminal, and influenced always by the body and its desires.

Chapter 19

Sleep

I want you to understand that I have not by any means explored the possibilities of the subliminal self in that little essay of mine. Please regard it merely as a preliminary canter. I have been puzzled as to the treatment of it.

When I was a dead man, that is to say when I was alive on earth, I believed that sleep was simply a withdrawal of the spirit, an emptying of the chambers of the brain and a search for refreshment in another world, or, rather, that there was a replenishing of spiritual energy, a kind of irrigation, and that from it there came that freshness, that sense of invigoration, which we have all experienced on waking to a new day. I believed firmly in a life passed in two worlds, and in this I was perfectly right. I was puzzled as to the exact conditions obtained during slumber, now I am more sensible of them. Actually the nerve-soul is detached from the body when you are in the state you call sleep. That means there is no direct interpreter, or medium, between the spirit and the brain cells. This is important. The body, as I have previously stated, is largely dominated by this nerve-soul. It becomes almost quiescent when the latter is withdrawn into a metetheric atmosphere. The nerve-soul is bathed in this atmosphere, and receives a very necessary stimulus, or rather nourishment, from what I believe you now call ether. But ether is a broad term, and it is in reality a subdivision of ether that feeds the nerve-soul during sleep. Perhaps I should coin a new word and call it "Etheric Essence." I feel I am most audacious in thus infringing on the rights of physicists, who alone should christen the elements—both visible and invisible. Now, while the nerve-soul is absent, the spirit is still close to the body. It cannot send the image— as I have termed it—directly to the brain. It makes no effort to do so usually, but there are occasions when the higher nerve centres are in a particularly susceptible state. Then the spirit may endeavour to cast upon it some image, or rather to direct one, through invoking a residuum of power that has been left behind by the nerve-soul. Then your sleeper will dream, perhaps, of some future event, or will image some violent death that is taking place elsewhere. The spirit draws within it the reflection of certain emotional affinities of the being who is slumbering and it thus succeeds on rare occasions in casting an image of the future, or of some present happening, upon the quiescent brain.

Now, you may ask me to explain the origin of the foolish, and apparently chaotic, dreams that visit the sleeper nightly. These, if you have the key, are neither foolish nor chaotic. Very often there is a steady nerve— irritation during the day, a firm suppression of emotions. This leads, on occasions, to the photographing of some of the causes of irritation, and these photos or pictures are bound to the neurons that have been active during the day. They (the pictures) are in a web of threads. There is no controlling entity, but the nerves can, and do, react upon them, making confused and foolish patterns. They are in every sense of the word nerve-visions, and must not be regarded as reflections emanating from a higher source.

I have defined attention as the direction of nervous energy into certain special cells of the brain. Now, if this flow has been violent and prolonged during waking hours, the vibration will continue. The echoes, as it were, of that concentration will still be resounding, but mingling with other echoes, other impressions, and these make a certain sequence that, at times, is added to by some very old associations. During the day, perhaps, you have seen a bonnet that reminded you of a dead grandmother. The actual reminder may be faint, but it will be sufficient to stir the thread that binds an old association to your brain cell. When control is relaxed, and sleep comes, the image of your grandmother figures in your dream. She has been drawn on to the canvas, through the visioning of a bonnet, some hours before. As the memory was of old times, it was far from the seat of operations, and the passage of time was necessary before it could arrive.

I fear I am writing in a rather dull fashion, but what I want to indicate is that the memories, the images of them, and the nerves, play a game of hide-and-seek with each other within the brain during sleep.

The spirit cannot send the controlling image, nor can that fluid shape, with its agglomeration of experiences, exert itself in the management of the vast population in the brain. I know also that, if the nerves are brittle or in a high state of tension, it is possible for them to be to a certain degree guided by a minor consciousness. But, though this entity gives the impulse of movement, it must obey the nerves which dominate, and owing to some harassing and latent memory compel the sleeper to arise and walk. This will account for sleep-walking usually. The nerves control the minor consciousness instead of the latter controlling them. But usually this psychic entity has just sufficient power to prevent the sleeper from falling into any great danger, or it can give the signal of alarm to the nerve-soul, and cause it to hurry back to the body again and assume control.

I have spoken of sleep in a rather crude manner, and I have endeavoured to show you that it is owing to the need of nourishment that the nerve-soul, or interpreter, has to withdraw and that this leads to an isolating process. The spirit can still animate the body; but only in very rare cases can it influence the directive centres in the brain, for its medium is absent. Undoubtedly during the hours of sleep a certain stratum of the subliminal self pervades the brain, or would seem to do so. What actually occurs is this. Certain old associations, old emotions, have been roused by events during the day. The nerve-soul has not allowed them to enter the active consciousness, it was busy with other matters. They have remained there, like a stream that is dammed up. The dam is removed, through the absence of the nerve-soul, and these memories, particularly if the nerves be in a state of tension, flood the field of the brain, and enter again the old frames, looking down once more on that interior where they had been, for a brief space, its decorations and the images of conscious thought.

I will speak very briefly about hypnosis. The large majority of hypnotised subjects are not hypnotised at all. But, if I may take a case of genuine hypnotism, I will show you that in one essential, at least, it differs from ordinary sleep. The nerve-soul of the subject is suspended, but it is not, save in a very extreme instance, absent from the body. It is not permitted to act. It forbids its own actions. That is an important point. The individual who hypnotises cannot, unless there is some morbid condition of the nerves, compel the individual to give up his will, that is to say, suspend the nerve-soul. Now the spirit, or subliminal self, is in a sense drawn nearer to the body through this suspension. Its creative flow no longer circulates, for it requires its medium and the latter is suspended. But another stratum of the subliminal self can be, and is often, summoned. I refer principally to that section connected with buried memories. Now the command of the hypnotist sets in motion some of the fluid shape, some of the essence directed by the nerve-soul when it operates, it, too, being a part of that invisible fluid body. A portion of its essence is used, merely in order that certain sunken memories may be drawn to the surface. They could not come if the nerve-soul were actively operating in conjunction with the image sent by the subliminal self. Actually hypnotism opens up a more direct road to the subliminal mind, that is to say, that part of it which is loose and floating. The Unifying Principle, the centre that sends the message when the ordinary consciousness is operating, is also out of touch when its medium is suspended.

You will understand, therefore, that a part only of the subliminal self can be drawn on by the subject.

Chapter 20

Telepathy

May I give you my opinion as regards telepathy between the living? It is different in some respects from telepathy from the dead. There must be a far greater adjustment on our side than when the two subjects are alive. However, we are perfectly conscious of our inner mind, so, on the whole, it is simpler for us. If you were more fully aware of your deeper mind it would become quite easy for you to act as a receiver or as a transmitter. But let me try and explain. I have already spoken of a fluid body which links up the sub-conscious mind with the physical body. Now, this fluid shape, as I shall call it, is constantly changing, it has an elasticity quite foreign to the physical body. It is decidedly impressionable, amazingly sensitive. The trouble is that it is not intimately connected with the brain; or, rather, the human being does not understand how to make that connection. He can do so partly by detaching his mind from certain matters so that the actual mechanism is not working at top speed. It can also be ma-nipulated in another way. Now, there is memory in relation to the flu-id. It can be tapped through 'the fluid. The fluid can also receive what you call the telepathic message. It does indeed receive many of them, but only in the case of certain rare human beings can the telepathic record be conveyed to the brain. I want to make clear that the fluid launches a message into space. It is not carried usually by any entity, but there are many floating filaments of mind which help to draw it into the fluid on which it makes the impression that may be conveyed from it to the brain.

The scientist seems to believe that no physiological or physical means can explain telepathy between the living. I say that the physiology of the soul can explain it. That would at first sight seem a contradiction in terms, but actually it is not quite the case. There are infinitesimal particles not yet discovered by human beings. They are so minute that you would not recognize them as matter. But to the dead, who have far finer perceptions, these particles are suggestive of matter though they cannot be said to resemble matter in most particulars. Anyway, these tiny atoms are influenced by emotion and will. These give a driving force to the atoms, the brain can give them the shape in which they are received.

The nerve-soul or the nerve-memory is, naturally, very much influenced by the consciousness. I have already told you that it responds very rapidly to stimuli. Very well, the consciousness braces itself for an effort. It desires to catch the thought sent by the agent when you arrange a telepathic experiment. That mere desire has, with many people, the effect of stiffening the nerve-soul into a kind of stillness. In that condition it is motionless. It cannot receive. The brain has sent an instinctive warning to it not to receive. In this case instinct conquers the conscious desire. It is the instinct that protects the individual against the inroads of alien thought. In its essence it is a right one. If you kept perpetually registering the thoughts of others a very unwholesome condition of brain might develop. Nature, therefore, gives the human being this protection from the many arrows of thought that might pierce the armour of consciousness and injure the mechanism. If a human being has this instinct sufficiently controlled he is likely to prove receptive. The nerve-memory or nerve-soul is, of course, very directly connected with the inner mind which plays its part in the reception of a telepathic message.

The term "fluid" must not be taken in its literal sense. I would not have used such a word in this connection when on earth. But now, for the sake of simplicity, and because the nerve-soul or shape is suggestive of something that flows, I employ this term which, at least, is suggestive and not in any respect technical.

Neither must the words I have employed in connection with the planes be taken literally. They are symbolic of those particular states.

Chapter 21

The Interpenetration of Thought Between the Two Worlds

There is continual interpenetration of thought between the visible and invisible worlds and that is what makes communication with you all the more difficult. If we could separate and classify the vast accumulation of floating thought from the living and the dead it would be far more easy then, with the way clear, to send you one easy flow of thought from one individual discarnate mind. It is possible to get lost in the vast forest of men's fancies, more particularly when you go out as a discarnate explorer. You are pretty sure to pick up false trails and in the end to give up the soluble problem in disgust. I speak not alone of minds but of the continual currents of thought thrown out by such millions tossed through our mighty Mother, the Universe, whose illimitable womb harbours them all.

I beg of you to remember that I am but a fallible shade. However, it is well in this difficult matter to lay down as our foundation certain premises. Firstly, let us take, for example, the average educated man. It is possible for him, while in the physical body, and while he is at the zenith of his mental power, to enter three states which differ very considerably from one another: first, the condition of deep sleep; second, the subjective state; third, the state of ordinary consciousness. You must allow much latitude for the subjective condition. It can vary to a wide degree. It may be induced by artificial means, through hypnotism. A subject well trained to respond to the hypnotist will, as you are aware, perform amazing feats, recall memories of early childhood, be insensible to pain, and, I believe, even obtain, at times, knowledge that appears to be of a wholly supernormal character. The Indian mystic can enter very easily into the subjective state and can, at times, learn of the doings of strangers who are many miles away from him. He can, in short, make mental journeys.

Now, in our life—the life of the so-called dead—there are three states also, though it cannot be said that they closely resemble the three orders of consciousness that prevail for man. Even when asleep you are, in a sense, conscious, sometimes more so than when you are in this subjective state, for pain or noise may rouse you, whereas the deeply entranced man may not feel pain, may not be even roused by thunder. When we discarnate beings desire to communicate through some sensitive we enter a dream or subjective state. There are two degrees of it that are important in relation to ourselves. If we are but slightly entranced we are detached from the memory of concrete facts in our past life. Further, if we communicate directly through the medium, though we often retain our personality, our manner of speech, we are frequently unable to communicate through the medium's hand or voice many exact facts about our past career on earth, sometimes not even our own names.

We can enter into the deeper mind of the medium and read many of the memories belonging to him, which are outside the cells, or neurons, being joined to them by invisible threads.

Now, you are aware of the strange association of ideas. You met a Mr. Tom Jones at a tea party ten years ago. You had forgotten all about him, even his name, but someone mentions it to you: At that moment it means nothing, perhaps, but in a minute or two you remember the Mr. Tom Jones you met ten years ago at a tea party. In the same manner the discarnate being may find certain memories in the subconsciousness of the medium which will recall certain facts connected with his past earth life. Then the memory is rapidly communicated.

I would now speak of the second degree of trance which may be penetrated by the discarnate being. It is a pleasant and, at times, very happy state. It is nearer to the condition of sleep and dreams than the one I have previously mentioned. When we are on this plane of consciousness we can enter the subjective mind of man. But it is necessary that he should come to our aid in this respect. He must either be closely bound to us by ties of affection or he must be what you call "psychic." Very well, those dear friends or relatives, who through their affection or love, or intense interest in us, conjure us up in their subjective thought, open the door to us dreaming shades, and we enter again into the earth dream. We perceive pictures of actual earth hap-penings, imprinting themselves on the subconscious mind of the one who has cleared the way for us, bridged the chasm with their love or their intense interest. Often we perceive most trivial incidents mirrored on their subconsciousness. Sometimes, when we are really thoroughly submerged in this dream atmosphere, we can get into touch not alone with one subconscious mind but with the subconscious mind of many thousands. It is like a wide sea stretching out before us. Much of it is scarcely apprehended. We can only tap it here and there, but, with the assistance of the guide we may draw out of this sea of mind the par-ticular association of ideas that corresponds with a happening, a name, or a place in our earth life. We recognize it and use it as evidence of identity when we are communicating.

Now, the third subjective state leads us to the Great Memory, but, alas, it is not the condition or state in which we approach our people on earth. We can gather up many of our memories when we thus reach out into the vast subconscious—or rather Superconscious—mind of the race. So I will not dwell upon this aspect at any great length beyond re-marking that those who have been among discarnate beings for many ages, those who are highly developed, the possessors of wisdom among us, can, on very rare occasions, while in the third state, communicate through a sensitive the actual history recorded in the Great Memory. But such beings are not suffered to communicate their own wisdom, for it cannot be expressed in terms of language, only an echo being sometimes caught which is rendered in the form of the inspired utter-ance of genius. Nevertheless, discarnate beings, who have only been a few years absent from the earth, in many cases cannot enter into this third subjective condition when they use the physical mechanism in order to give their thoughts to the world.

It is true that we communicate by pictures or images, by signs which the deeper mind of the sensitive apprehends, and sometimes we may convey, by a sign or symbol, a name or word unknown to the medium. It would be well for you to note that what you call "normal conscious-ness" means the raising up of the barriers between your mind and an-other man's mind. But behind all that there is among human beings a deeper self, a subjective mentality that can trespass into the domain of other subliminal selves, that meets with few barriers. This matter, however, belongs to another story.

I would ask you not to be troubled by my remark that when discar-nate beings pursue an active, eager life here the greater part of their concrete memories are temporarily in abeyance. Mark you, they are in a state of normal psychic consciousness under such circumstances. But a discarnate son and father, or any others who have dear remembrance of one another, may, if they so desire, recapture all their old memories of facts in their earth life if they choose to enter the third subjective state together. Then these two discarnate beings can re-enact, if they will, the drama of their earth career page by page. They can recall all the infinitesimal knowledge they reaped with such care on earth. Homer, *The Odyssey*, all the painfully acquired Greek and Latin of school boy days, recollections of youthful games, of hoarded learning may be gathered anew in all clearness. The very conversations at tea tables or at dull dinner parties can be recalled and digested, perhaps with some boredom again. You can gather to you all the old rusty relics, all the little quarrels and worries, all your proudly gotten learning if that is your desire. But you must, of course, enter, with your friend or relative, into the third subjective state if you yearn to play again the old roles in the past, if you would wistfully finger once more the precious little details of circumstance and happenings in your earth life, if you would, indeed, be like some old man or woman who takes from their drawer ancient love-letters, lockets of hair, and little miniatures framed in gold which recall dear departed days.

But many of us are of an adventurous temperament. It amuses us, for a while, to dally with these pages in the *Book of Life*, and from them, when we meet our loved ones after death, we derive a certain wistful pleasure, or a quiet delight, without the pangs of the flesh attached to them. We tire, however, after a very brief while, of these heaped-up remains of our past careers, all so carefully stored in the Great Granary. We would pass from out one fold of time into another; we would be bold and adventure into the imagination of God. So, while in this third subjective state, we turn again the pages of the *Book of Life* and read the future of our race. We gaze upon a drama that has not yet been enacted upon the earth, the vague echo of which is sometimes caught by prophets and soothsayers. We perceive the wanderings of those begotten by us, the fate of those who are of our blood, who bear upon their foreheads the seal of kinship with us. And, indeed, many of us sorrowfully close the Book of Life when we have thus gazed into a future that is not yet for men, sprung out of the Unknown, out of the boundless sea, which, I must again remind you, is the creation of the all-pervading imagination of God.

Finally, the power to enter the third subjective state and thus to follow the future as well as the past, page by page, is bestowed only upon those souls whom human beings—to use a trite adjective—would call "advanced" or would hail as "spiritually developed." Many millions of souls, who have passed through the Gates of Death, rest within the borders and limitations of their own psychic development. I use the word "psychic" here in the general sense, not in its relation to the study of survival after death. Such myriad souls follow a road and a destiny that does not, as a rule, lead them for a time, at least, to the great super-conscious mind of the earth. These so-called dead remain in spheres and states of pleasant—or sometimes disagreeable—illusion. I cannot write concerning all the souls who pass to an invisible life from the arms of their foster mother-earth.

Chapter 22

Happiness For the Average Man and Woman

In discussing happiness it is necessary to have a sense of proportion and to classify human beings. The life that brings true and permanent joy to one will bring only discontent and positive distress to another.

Learned men have endeavoured to declare hard-and-fast principles of happiness and in so doing have worked on a false premise. Infinite is the variety of human nature. You cannot say to any class, nation, man or race, "Follow the principles I have imparted to you and you will discover happiness." The individual or nation in question may not be in a sufficiently developed state physically, mentally, and spiritually to be capable of applying such principles to their daily life, or, if they are capable, the principles may be so framed that the promised happiness resolves itself into boredom or acute disillusionment.

For instance, the Christian and Buddhist ascetics and mystics are in accord as to the road to happiness. They will assure you that no true happiness can be derived from the use of the senses, neither can it be obtained by money or by power and authority over others. They recommend complete renunciation, scorn of wealth, power, beauty, in whatsoever way it expresses itself. They claim that true happiness can be found only in contemplation, in communion with God—in contempt of all those works of God which please the senses or satisfy natural desires.

I am afraid their views are open to many and serious objections. For the mystic, perhaps, this inner life consists of the only real happiness. But ninety men out of a hundred are not mystics, they belong to a general pattern and are constitutionally incapable of putting such recommendations into practice, or, if they attempt to do so, they merely warp, limit, and embitter their natures.

True happiness for the average man is to be found in such words as moderation, self-control, and freedom. He must first learn to control himself, and, that power once acquired, he must learn to control people and situations wisely. Thus he wins his freedom. Second, Tom Jones has to gain some knowledge of his own unimportance in the prevailing scheme of things. Third, he should cultivate any special creative power he may possess.

Now, his control of himself gives to him a certain serenity, so that daily worries and misfortunes fail to penetrate—fail to upset his calm. His power to control other people will save him from physical distress, from destitution, and will enable him to defeat any persons who may, in various emotional ways, endeavour to turn his life into a hell. His sense of his own unimportance will, in itself, bring happiness by leading him naturally to throw himself into other people's lives, so that "self" can be temporarily forgotten and a lively sympathy extended where it is genuinely needed.

Now, the creative instinct is an essential part of a man's nature. Its wise expression should be one of his principal preoccupations. It springs, partly, from the sex urge, but often offers the greatest happiness in activities quite apart from sex. Whatever a man's sex life, he would be wise if he sought in some way or other for an outlet for the creative principle. If he has not a constructive mind or imagination he can express it merely in the enjoyment of beauty in some form or other, in a wise but controlled indulgence of his senses. But happy is the man with self-control as well as real creative power, however humble may be the medium of its expression.

Usually, the ascetic who recommends you to scorn money has no anxieties on that score. Either his friends or admirers supply him with all he needs or he has an excellent income of his own.

I therefore strongly advise the seeker of happiness to have a due appreciation of money. Without it he must starve or experience such physical discomfort, such ill-health, that he is unable to keep the light of his intelligence or soul bright within its temple. He is no longer free because, hourly, the clamorous needs of the body besiege him, and if he is employed for long hours at a small wage he has no time or physical strength for the cultivation of his own nature or for the enjoyment he can give to others through its fruition.

A desire for money in moderation is a virtue, for it happens to be a desire to become a complete man, and, through such completion and its resultant content, to benefit others.

Happiness comes through effort; through a wise and controlled indulgence in the pleasures of the senses; through athletic activities for the perfecting of the body; through study for the development of the mind; and through toleration or a charitable outlook. The development of these leads to the cultivation of the spirit.

True happiness will be found by the average man in the constant and wise use of all his talents, all his powers—of body, senses, mind, and spiritual perception.

Lastly, in wisdom will the modern human being find the secret of life and the secret of serenity. Faith, hope, and charity—all these virtues commended by St. Paul—are contained within this lofty word and all are made lovely by its radiance. For faith, hope, and charity without wisdom are without light, and things that are hidden in darkness may not attain to healthy growth.

[Unfinished, owing to illness of G. C.]

Chapter 23

God is Greater Than Love

I t is strange to me that God should be described as loving and good, or as jealous and vengeful. He is none of these. He is the inevitable, the "Omega" of all life. But He is neither evil nor good, neither cruel nor kind. He is the Purpose behind all purpose. He neither loves nor hates, there is no thought created that expresses Him, for He would seem to me to be all creation and yet apart from it. He is the Idea behind the myriad worlds, behind the unnumbered Universes.

When we speak of love and hate we think in human terms. Perhaps we picture to ourselves the beautiful love of a mother for her son; we think of a man who loves his wife devotedly; we think of heroic deeds performed for the sake of love. Then we visualise hatred—our loathing of some individual who has tricked us, deceived us, or committed some rather evil crime.

Now, neither human love nor human hate even at their highest can be regarded as qualities possessed by God. For in all love as we know it there is some taint, some streak of desire. Therefore love is not of a purity which we can associate with God. And even the noblest hatred has in it some soil, so that we blaspheme if we couple it with the Name of God.

There is, in short, no phrase that we can apply to God in this connection. We might say, "He is infinite compassion, infinite tenderness"; but he is not the "loving Father" as described by the prayer book. He is something loftier and grander. "A loving Father"—in the sense the world uses the word—loves only his own. In a war, for instance, the

English will claim God's love as their particular property, the Germans will claim it as theirs. Always man uses the term "love" when he wishes to imply that it is a devotion for certain selected persons or selected things. He may mechanically say that God loves everything He has created, but he is utterly unable to understand such a condition of mind, so this phrase is meaningless from his point of view. I would not cheapen the idea of the Creator by calling Him a God of love. For, inevitably, I should be limiting our conception of God; I should reduce Him to human terms; I would, in short, make a man of Him.

No, God does not love. For love is a human virtue that is like a flame, that leaps up and down, that at one moment in life may be a glory; but when there are many moments the glory cannot be maintained, and love becomes, even with the best of men and women, tainted by irritability, by some peevishness, or by some selfish melancholy.

God does not change. His fatherhood and motherhood of the Universe never falter, never fail. If He were love, then the marvellous creation of the life you know would never have continued so perfectly. It would have been subject to the changeable character of that thing you call love. At times there might have been cessation of growth—great harvests destroyed, vast tracts of country laid waste because the heavens did not continue to gather moisture. Tides might have spread themselves over half the visible earth, mountains leaped from their rocky seats, many millions of living creatures suddenly perishing. I tell you that if God possessed love, as man understands and knows it, the history of the world would have been wholly changed, changed rather for evil than for good. God is greater than love. That is the phrase you should utter.

I know that our Master, Christ, preached to the Jews, saying "God is love." And to Christ God was love. For Christ set no human meaning to the term as has been the way with every soul who has walked upon this earth since the world began. The claim that Jesus was the Son of God is based upon the fact that He was the one unique Son of Man who knew the mystery of God, who, in saying "God is love," alone of all men understood what He meant by that phrase.

All sons and daughters of Adam, when they declare that "God is love," mean by it love in the human sense: for it is all that they understand and know. So I would counsel finite minds to endeavour to image the Deity in the phrase, "God is greater than love."

THE END

94

Paperbacks also available from
White Crow Books

Elsa Barker—*Letters from
a Living Dead Man*
ISBN 978-1-907355-83-7

Elsa Barker—*War Letters from
the Living Dead Man*
ISBN 978-1-907355-85-1

Elsa Barker—*Last Letters from
the Living Dead Man*
ISBN 978-1-907355-87-5

Richard Maurice Bucke—
Cosmic Consciousness
ISBN 978-1-907355-10-3

Arthur Conan Doyle—
The Edge of the Unknown
ISBN 978-1-907355-14-1

Arthur Conan Doyle—
The New Revelation
ISBN 978-1-907355-12-7

Arthur Conan Doyle—
The Vital Message
ISBN 978-1-907355-13-4

Arthur Conan Doyle with
Simon Parke—*Conversations
with Arthur Conan Doyle*
ISBN 978-1-907355-80-6

Meister Eckhart with Simon Parke—
Conversations with Meister Eckhart
ISBN 978-1-907355-18-9

D. D. Home—*Incidents in my Life Part 1*
ISBN 978-1-907355-15-8

Mme. Dunglas Home; edited,
with an Introduction, by Sir
Arthur Conan Doyle—*D. D.
Home: His Life and Mission*
ISBN 978-1-907355-16-5

Edward C. Randall—
Frontiers of the Afterlife
ISBN 978-1-907355-30-1

Rebecca Ruter Springer—
Intra Muros: My Dream of Heaven
ISBN 978-1-907355-11-0

Leo Tolstoy, edited by Simon
Parke—*Forbidden Words*
ISBN 978-1-907355-00-4

Leo Tolstoy—*A Confession*
ISBN 978-1-907355-24-0

Leo Tolstoy—*The Gospel in Brief*
ISBN 978-1-907355-22-6

Leo Tolstoy—*The Kingdom
of God is Within You*
ISBN 978-1-907355-27-1

Leo Tolstoy—*My Religion:
What I Believe*
ISBN 978-1-907355-23-3

Leo Tolstoy—*On Life*
ISBN 978-1-907355-91-2

Leo Tolstoy—*Twenty-three Tales*
ISBN 978-1-907355-29-5

Leo Tolstoy—*What is Religion
and other writings*
ISBN 978-1-907355-28-8

Leo Tolstoy—*Work While
Ye Have the Light*
ISBN 978-1-907355-26-4

Leo Tolstoy—*The Death of Ivan Ilyich*
ISBN 978-1-907661-10-5

Leo Tolstoy—*Resurrection*
ISBN 978-1-907661-09-9

Leo Tolstoy with Simon Parke—
Conversations with Tolstoy
ISBN 978-1-907355-25-7

Howard Williams with an Introduction
by Leo Tolstoy—*The Ethics of Diet:
An Anthology of Vegetarian Thought*
ISBN 978-1-907355-21-9

Vincent Van Gogh with Simon
Parke—*Conversations with Van Gogh*
ISBN 978-1-907355-95-0

Wolfgang Amadeus Mozart with Simon
Parke—*Conversations with Mozart*
ISBN 978-1-907661-38-9

Jesus of Nazareth with Simon Parke—
Conversations with Jesus of Nazareth
ISBN 978-1-907661-41-9

Thomas à Kempis with Simon
Parke—*The Imitation of Christ*
ISBN 978-1-907661-58-7

Julian of Norwich with Simon
Parke—*Revelations of Divine Love*
ISBN 978-1-907661-88-4

Allan Kardec—*The Spirits Book*
ISBN 978-1-907355-98-1

Allan Kardec—*The Book on Mediums*
ISBN 978-1-907661-75-4

Emanuel Swedenborg—*Heaven and Hell*
ISBN 978-1-907661-55-6

P.D. Ouspensky—*Tertium Organum:
The Third Canon of Thought*
ISBN 978-1-907661-47-1

Dwight Goddard—*A Buddhist Bible*
ISBN 978-1-907661-44-0

Michael Tymn—*The Afterlife Revealed*
ISBN 978-1-970661-90-7

Michael Tymn—*Transcending the
Titanic: Beyond Death's Door*
ISBN 978-1-908733-02-3

Guy L. Playfair—*If This Be Magic*
ISBN 978-1-907661-84-6

Guy L. Playfair—*The Flying Cow*
ISBN 978-1-907661-94-5

Guy L. Playfair —*This House is Haunted*
ISBN 978-1-907661-78-5

Carl Wickland, M.D.—
Thirty Years Among the Dead
ISBN 978-1-907661-72-3

John E. Mack—*Passport to the Cosmos*
ISBN 978-1-907661-81-5

Peter & Elizabeth Fenwick—
The Truth in the Light
ISBN 978-1-908733-08-5

Erlendur Haraldsson—
Modern Miracles
ISBN 978-1-908733-25-2

Erlendur Haraldsson—
At the Hour of Death
ISBN 978-1-908733-27-6

Erlendur Haraldsson—
The Departed Among the Living
ISBN 978-1-908733-29-0

Brian Inglis—*Science and Parascience*
ISBN 978-1-908733-18-4

Brian Inglis—*Natural and Supernatural:
A History of the Paranormal*
ISBN 978-1-908733-20-7

Ernest Holmes—*The Science of Mind*
ISBN 978-1-908733-10-8

Victor Zammit—*Afterlife: A
Lawyer Presents the Evidence.*
ISBN 978-1-908733-22-1

Casper S. Yost—*Patience
Worth: A Psychic Mystery*
ISBN 978-1-908733-06-1

William Usborne Moore—
Glimpses of the Next State
ISBN 978-1-907661-01-3

William Usborne Moore—
The Voices
ISBN 978-1-908733-04-7

John W. White—
The Highest State of Consciousness
ISBN 978-1-908733-31-3

Stafford Betty—
The Imprisoned Splendor
ISBN 978-1-907661-98-3

Paul Pearsall, Ph.D. —
Super Joy
ISBN 978-1-908733-16-0

**All titles available as eBooks, and selected titles available in Hardback and
Audiobook formats from www.whitecrowbooks.com**

Lightning Source UK Ltd.
Milton Keynes UK
UKOW051440150713

213814UK00001B/50/P